GOOD
MEN

GOOD MEN

A PRACTICAL HANDBOOK
FOR DIVORCED DADS

JACK FEUER

AVON BOOKS  NEW YORK

AVON BOOKS
A division of
The Hearst Corporation
1350 Avenue of the Americas
New York, New York 10019

Copyright © 1997 by Jack Feuer
Front cover photograph by David Stoecklein/The Stock Market
Inside back cover author photograph by Martine Malle
Published by arrangement with the author
Visit our website at http://www.AvonBooks.com
ISBN: 0-380-78398-3

Library of Congress Cataloging in Publication Data:

Feuer, Jack.
  Good men : a practical handbook for divorced dads / [Jack Feuer].
    p.   cm.
Includes index.
1. Divorced fathers—United States—Handbooks, manuals, etc. 2. Father and child—United States—Handbooks, manuals, etc. 3. Divorce—United States—Handbooks, manuals, etc. I. Title.
HQ756.F48 1997   97-20509
306.89—dc21   CIP

First Avon Books Trade Printing: November 1997

AVON TRADEMARK REG. U.S. PAT. OFF. AND IN OTHER COUNTRIES, MARCA REGIS-TRADA, HECHO EN U.S.A.

Printed in the U.S.A.

OPM   10 9 8 7 6 5 4 3 2 1

For Alex, of course, who taught me that there is nothing in the universe more powerful than the love between a father and his son.

So many good men and women graciously gave their time, their talent or simply just shared their stories for this book. Thanks to my agent, Jane Dystel and my editor, Rachel Klayman, for refusing to accept anything less than the best book I could write. To Cliff Scott, Bill Bartshe, Philly Murtha, Bea Campodonico, Toni and Jeffrey Lattimer, Linda and Devin Clark, and Toni Lopopolo, who helped me get on with it. To all the fathers and mothers, divorced or otherwise, who gave me insight into the mysterious art of parenting. To Alex's mom, Livia Eden, for the other side. And finally, to the children of divorce, for loving us in spite of it all.

Table of Contents

GOOD MEN

Foreword:
The Uncivil War

> I had married once "till death do us part"—and it
> had turned out not to be that durable.
>
> —ROBERT A. HEINLEIN

Every thirteen seconds, another marriage ends in America.
One million divorces every year. Overall, four out of every
ten first marriages will end in divorce, and Americans are
even worse at remarriage—six out of every ten second marriages fail.

Why?

It's politically popular to declare our nation's high divorce
rate a portent of the end of civilization. According to this
theory, the high incidence of failed marriages is the result of
a decadent nation, the inevitable product of an "anything
goes" popular culture that makes a virtue of selfishness.
Wrong.

Divorce is rarely, if ever, an act of personal selfishness on the part of parents. Quite the contrary. There isn't a single father or mother in this country who got divorced just for the hell of it. There's nothing casual about breaking up a family. People don't do it because they're bored or restless or selfish. Divorce is what people do when they have no other choice.

Divorcing parents don't think breaking up is "okay." It's not just another lifestyle "option." Divorce represents a failure, and nobody feels that burden more heavily than the families of divorce themselves. Breaking up a family is an agonizing life choice good men and women feel they must make, sometimes precisely for the sake of their children.

I speak from firsthand experience. Before my wife and I made the excruciating decision to divorce, we had gone through two trial separations, two years of counseling, and daily bouts of agony discussing just how we might save our marriage. We finally were forced to accept the extraordinarily painful fact that we couldn't.

Once we'd made that decision, we had to figure out how to make our new lives work. There were two things we definitely agreed on: (1) we both wanted to do what was best for our son, Alex; and (2) Alex needed both of his parents.

More divorcing parents, judges, and experts need to realize this: if children are going to survive a divorce intact and grow into mentally healthy, functioning adults, they need both their mothers and their fathers in their lives.

Divorce is a traumatic, world-shaking event in the life of a family—but it is *not* a death knell. Divorce can be—and is—not only endured but overcome. Everyone in a divorced family can survive and even prosper as long as each person understands what is happening and takes appropriate action.

To do that, of course, the families of divorce need information. The parents and the kids who do the best are the ones who seek out, find, and take advantage of resources that can help them reconstruct their lives and relationships. The divorced families who make it are those who understand they can't go it alone.

If you're female and divorced in America, you're in luck. Plenty of postmarriage help is readily available to you all across the country—there's no end of useful places for divorced mothers to turn to. The children of divorce have just as many organizations, therapists, books, and programs. Even stepfamilies can find dozens of groups, books, and allies.

If you're a divorced dad, though, forget it.

Very few resources exist, outside the political action groups, that are specifically designed to help a divorced father. There's practically nothing to prepare him for life after marriage, let alone to equip him to handle it well, especially when it comes to parenting. This is the great irony of divorce in America, because of all the members of a sundered family, including children, fathers are the least able (or willing, perhaps) to understand that divorce is something people absolutely cannot handle by themselves.

Shortly after I was divorced in 1990, I asked my therapist if she knew of any organizations that could help me with my number one divorced-dad goal: building a healthy relationship with my son, Alex, who was just over two years old at the time.

"Divorced fathers?" my therapist muttered, looking puzzled. She turned to her desk and picked up a thick book that listed support groups. For several minutes, she riffled through it, looking more perplexed with each page. Finally she closed the book and said, "Well, I think there's one. It's not quite what you're looking for, but call them. Maybe they can help."

Uh-huh. "What about groups for divorced women?" I asked.

"Oh, yes," she said. "Hundreds."

That's not right. Divorced fathers face a daunting gauntlet of emotional, social, economic, and psychological challenges. Yet there remain few avenues of support.

George Handley, a therapist in Michigan whose experiences as a noncustodial divorced dad affected him so deeply that he geared his entire practice to working with divorced men, says that when he started his practice in the mid-1980s, he had to base his counseling on "my experience and the experience of other people I knew in the same position. There was just no information on this. And I don't think the resources are any different now."

Some divorce organizations offer guidance as part of a broader mandate, as do divorced-dad encounter groups and fathers' groups concerned with legal rights. But there is no one organization specifically and exclusively for divorced fathers and all aspects of their lives.

Many books on the general consequences of divorce have been written by psychologists, sociologists, and ex-government bureaucrats. Books on the psychological aspects of divorce. Books on the effects of divorce on children. Books on the religious aspects of divorce. Guides to divorce laws. And my personal favorite: *Cannibals, Witches & Divorce.*

But if any of these works single out the experience of being a divorced dad—most do not—they make only incomplete passes at the subject, concentrating on divorce laws, parenting realities, or psychology, but never all three. In addition, almost all of these works are written by women, many of them custodial mothers, and their insight into the plight of divorced fathers is often sketchy at best.

The same pattern predominates in the anecdotal record. The library shelves are filled with first-person accounts written by divorced mothers. By contrast, I don't even need all the fingers of one hand to count the number of similar books I found by divorced fathers, and that's after several years of determined digging.

It's true that some elements of divorced parenting are universal, but men face many specific challenges in postdivorce parenting that get little or no attention. The most obvious problem we face, of course, is handling the overwhelming emotions of divorce. American men, by and large, are still not trained to express or handle strong emotions. But divorced men face more tangible challenges every day—even modern dads usually don't know how to cook very well, or when to take their sniffling toddler to the doctor, or even how to potty train. We have little or no help in formulating a postdivorce parenting approach that takes into account our special needs as divorced fathers. How do we keep on being dads when we live hundreds of miles away from our kids, for example? How do we make our children feel that our home is their home even though they stay with us only a small percentage of the time?

These kinds of questions and many others like them prompted me to write this book. As a journalist who reports on cultural change, I was naturally drawn to a subject with such enormous impact on the most basic element of American society. But if your beat is the *zeitgeist*, you are always part of the story, so *Good Men* also springs from my own need as a divorced dad for information and good counsel.

In the following pages readers will find true stories of how men, women, and children have forged strong and healthy lives for themselves after divorce. *Good Men* is intended as a resource for every person caught up in America's uncivil war, but the invisible men, damaged by the conflict—the "you" this book refers to at every opportunity—are its main focus. Their point of view. Their problems. Their solutions. Divorced fathers will find themselves reflected in every anecdote, every suggestion, every expert's observation. (To protect their privacy, the names of most interviewees have been changed, except when they expressly gave permission to use their real names, or when their identities are important to understanding their stories.)

I also present the viewpoints of the divorce experts, of course. But this book will look further than the makers of studies, surveys, and statistical measurements. (Relying on researchers to discover the truth about anything can be perilous.) In addition, you'll find within these pages sound parenting advice from shrinks and lawyers, online experts, and even Captain Kangaroo.

I'll start with a brief history of divorce and custody issues, to help you understand just why the courts, judges, and media think the way they do about divorced dads. Maybe this information will help you secure better custody arrangements for your own children.

Most divorced men's experiences, naturally, fall somewhere between the extremes of total devotion to their kids and complete abrogation of their parental responsibility. Every divorced father is likely to be a bit of a "Disneyland Dad," for example (striving to delight and entertain his kids every hour of each visit), but he probably also disciplines, assigns chores, helps with homework during the time his kids stay with him, and does a lot of other day-to-day dad stuff as well. Similarly, most men are likely to find that their relationships with their ex-wives contain a little bit of both the good and the bad examples we investigate in the following chapters. No divorced dad has ever been nominated for sainthood: for instance, we all commit the cardinal sin of fighting with our ex-wives in front of our kids sometime or other.

This book does contain some divorced-dad horror stories, but they serve as cautionary reminders only. Nobody would be well-served by yet another enraged polemic.

For a few years I worked as an automotive journalist. During that time I heard car marketers, researchers, reporters, and analysts use the same two phrases over and over again: "things gone wrong," which were descriptions of the problems people had with their cars, and "things gone right," which were the features and characteristics that made people fall in love with the cars they drove—the things that worked.

Good Men is about "things gone right" in divorced-dad parenting.

In the end, divorce isn't really about fathers or mothers at all. It's about our future. It's about the children. It's about making peace in an uncivil war that makes victims of us all.

CHAPTER 1

◆

The Daddy Factor:
Playing a Part in Your Child's Life

Daddies count . . . a lot.

—JAMES CARVILLE

The nuclear family may be the best way to raise a child—but it's not the only way. The reality is, families do break up. Or, to paraphrase the famous bumper sticker, "Divorce happens." It's been happening almost as long as marriage has been happening. And it will continue to happen. When it does, it's the responsibility of the parents involved to rise above their differences, as serious as they may be, and work together for the benefit of their children.

One of the first things divorced parents must agree on is that children need to have both parents actively involved in their lives. This may prove to be a battle for divorced dads

1

because of a misinformed belief that dads (especially divorced dads) don't know how to parent. Not only is that not true, but, in fact, dads are such an integral part of a child's upbringing that their absence from a child's life can create serious problems.

To understand why our society, including lawyers, judges, and the media, seem to be anti–divorced dads, let's look back at the history of divorce and custody.

The concept of a legal procedure for ending a marriage is ancient—so old, in fact, that it's part of what many scholars believe was the first written set of laws in human history: the Code of Hammurabi, named after the great Babylonian emperor who devised the code during his long reign (1792–1750 B.C.). Some historians say the modern world was born when human beings began to farm. Others argue that true civilization really began with this code, which included civilization's first requirement for written marriage contracts. It also provided a mechanism for divorce—including provisions for the payment of alimony and child support.

In Hammurabi's days, Babylonian wives (and husbands, supposedly) could obtain a divorce for desertion, cruelty, or neglect, but they didn't have to divorce their husbands for bigamy or adultery. Those were capital crimes for both husbands and wives, punishable by death.

And you thought you had it tough.

Pretechnological civilizations, as harsh as most of them were on females, many times softened on the subject of women and divorce. In the Egypt of the pharaohs, wives enjoyed the right to initiate divorce. In pre-Christian Rome, a husband and wife could end their marriage with nothing more than a formal letter. And among some Native American tribes, a woman could divorce her man by leaving his moccasins on the doorstep, a far more merciful gesture than maxing out the credit cards.

Religion, though, frequently took a dim view of divorce. Christian and Hindu strictures, for example, forbade the dissolution of a marriage altogether. In the West, the church did much to give divorce the taint of "sin" it continues to suffer from today. In heavily Catholic Ireland, divorce was considered a crime until 1995—and the vote in the referendum that legalized breaking up a marriage passed by a scant nine thousand votes, the closest election result in Irish history.

However, in most countries the view of divorce as a sin was challenged by other interpretations. Martin Luther decreed that divorce was a secular subject, "just like dress and food, home and field." And divorce was legalized in England by Henry VIII when he broke with the Roman Catholic Church and decreed that sundering a marriage no longer required an act of God.

It did, however, require a separate act of the House of Lords.

The Puritans brought divorce to the New World in the early 1600s, but in a foreshadowing of the confusion that enveloped family law in the United States, the colonists imported three different schools of thought on the subject: (1) the English monarchy's view that it was legal but governed by politicians; (2) the Protestant idea that divorce was secular and therefore a matter for the civil authorities, not the church; and (3) the traditional Roman Catholic point of view that marriage was permanent and unbreakable.

As for the federal government, the Constitution was silent on the subject of marriage and divorce and, despite several attempts to pass amendments, Congress never drafted any legislation on divorce. So every state was on its own with regard to family law legislation, including how it awarded custody of the children of divorce.

The Tender Years Trap

The word "custody" comes from the Latin *custos*, which means "guard." Roman children were a man's property, something to be "guarded," because they worked at home and consequently were important contributors to the family's economic health. And indeed, throughout most of history, family law presumed that the father was the primary parent, and therefore he automatically received sole custody if his marriage broke up. Early nineteenth-century feminists, in fact, targeted the presumption of male sole custody as one of their primary objections to the status quo.

With the advent of the Industrial Revolution in England in the latter part of the last century, however, the home lost its place as the center of the family's economic life. Mother and children were no longer pivotal to keeping bread on the table. Now Dad brought home the bread, usually by working in a factory.

Relieved of their responsibility as co-breadwinners (without, it should be noted, any input from them), mothers, of course, were still the nurturers, the primary caregivers for their children, as well as the keepers of the hearth. The female came to be viewed as the essential parent in a child's formative years (usually up to the age of six or so), and society accepted without question the primary role of the mother in a child's "tender years." By the end of the century, the custody tradition of most of human history had been turned completely around and women were almost always granted custody of their children in a divorce. Few men even thought to object—they had become imprisoned in the narrow parental role society forced them to play.

This philosophy, which came to be called the "Tender Years Doctrine," was the foundation upon which custody decisions were based in the United States. The U.S. legal precedent was set in a 1925 ruling that used the "best interests of the child" as a guideline for determining custody. That sounds equitable (it still is the concept by which family law courts in virtually every state are guided), but in a culture that rigidly defined men as breadwinners and women as nurturers, the Tender Years Doctrine was almost always anti-father in practice. And its malignant legacy lingers today.

The first time I met with my divorce lawyer, he immediately got busy calculating the amount of child support I would pay under California family law. Never once did he mention that I had any other options besides giving my wife sole custody of my son. After the divorce was settled, I asked him why he had given me no other alternatives, and he said so few fathers sought custody of their children, he automatically assumed they didn't want it unless they brought it up first.

Lately, though, cracks are beginning to show in the formidable anti-father fortress, especially in the area of custody. Determined bands of activists are launching persistent and growing attacks on the gender presumptions and legal traditions that have governed family law in the United States for more than a century.

Their cause has even acquired a name: the fathers' rights movement. And it is making a difference.

Divided They Stand

The seed that sprouted into the fathers' rights movement is generally considered the 1975 custody case of famed child psychologist Lee Salk. He fought for and won custody of his teenage son and ten-year-old daughter in a New York court, marking the beginning of a slow reappraisal of the nation's attitudes and legal proclivities toward custody and visitation.

Official support came rapidly from social scientists. Two years after Salk's custody case the American Psychological Association officially decreed that "it is scientifically and psychologically baseless, as well as a violation of human rights, to discriminate against men because of their sex in assignment of children's custody, in adoption, in the staffing of child-care services, and personnel practices providing for parental leave in relation to childbirth and emergencies involving children."

Thus emboldened and with a new resolve, good men began to gather in fathers' rights groups all across the country. Today one estimate puts the current number of fathers' rights organizations at 250, with a total of fifty thousand members. Some of these groups are dedicated to the male parent, like the United Fathers of America, based in Los Angeles; some have a broader mandate, like the National Congress for Men and Children, a coalition of fathers' rights groups based in Washington, D.C., and the Children's Rights Council (CRC), also based in the nation's capital, which unites parents and stepparents of both sexes, and even grandparents under its banner.

Spurred on by the activists, good men have engaged the Tender Years Doctrine and the cultural assumptions on which it is based in courtrooms, in statehouses, and even in the White House. The Children's Rights Council has been pounding on legislators' doors since it was founded in 1985, and is credited as the catalyst behind the 1988 Family Support Act, which authorized the first federal money ever allocated for visitation.

The CRC and other fathers' rights groups played pivotal roles in the creation of the Welfare Reform Working Group in 1992. Activists were part of the deliberations that created the U.S. Commission on Child and Family Welfare, which focuses on custody and visitation issues and which many fathers' rights groups believe is the government's first serious attempt to address fathers' issues. And a group of activists led by Bill Harrington, founder of the American Fathers Coalition, met in October 1993 with William Galston, President Clinton's deputy assistant for domestic policy. (In a personal tribute to good fathering, Galston resigned in 1995 to spend more time with his son.)

In the fall of 1995, the Children Youth and Family Consortium Electronic Clearinghouse distributed the following on the World Wide Web:

The White House
June 16, 1995

MEMORANDUM FOR THE HEADS OF EXECUTIVE DE-
PARTMENTS AND AGENCIES
Subject: Supporting the Role of Fathers in Families

I am firm in my belief that the future of our Republic
depends on strong families and that committed fathers
are essential to those families. I am also aware that
strengthening fathers' involvement with their children
cannot be accomplished by the Federal Government
alone; the solutions lie in the hearts and consciences of
individual fathers and the support of the families and
communities in which they live. However, there are ways
for a flexible, responsive Government to help support
men in their roles as fathers.

Therefore, today I am asking the Federal agencies to
assist me in this effort. I direct all executive departments
and agencies to review every program, policy, and initia-
tive (hereinafter referred to collectively as "programs")
that pertains to families to:

- ensure, where appropriate, and consistent with program objectives, that they seek to engage and meaning-
  fully include fathers;
- proactively modify those programs that were designed
  to serve primarily mothers and children, where appropriate and consistent with program objectives, to
  explicitly include fathers and strengthen their involvement with their children;
- include evidence of father involvement and participation, where appropriate, in measuring the success of
  the programs;
- and incorporate fathers, where appropriate, in government initiated research regarding children and their
  families.

William J. Clinton

Divorced dads who are also legislators are pursuing non-married fathers' rights in government with vigor. California State Senator Charles Calderon, for example, launched a drive to widen rights for California's unwed fathers after a successful but emotionally devastating court fight for joint custody of his two young sons that cost him $90,000. (A similar pattern exists in the social sciences, where a hefty percentage of psychologists, sociologists, and researchers studying divorce and its effects on children are themselves divorced parents.)

Pragmatic self-interest has helped convince legislators as well. Study after study proves that the more involved a father is, the more likely he is to pay child support in full and on time. In 1991 the U.S. Census Bureau reported that fathers with joint physical custody paid just over 90 percent of their child support, and fathers with visitation paid just under 80 percent. Fathers with neither joint custody nor visitation paid only 44.5 percent. Divorced dads with joint legal custody, which gives them the right to inquire about such things as their children's medical records or school situations but does not include physical custody of their kids, paid 90 percent or more of their child support.

Even on the most vicious of the uncivil war's fronts, our nation's courts, fathers can finally point to some victories. In New York City, TV producer Michael Krauss, ex-husband of *Good Morning America* personality Joan Lunden, demanded and received joint physical custody of his two daughters—quite an achievement considering New York's woeful record as a stalwart anti-father state. Just as remarkable is the fact that it was his divorce lawyer who encouraged Krauss to fight for the right to share parenting of his daughters.

This refreshing break from the traditional divorced male's reaction—glumly acquiescing to whatever custody or parenting policy is shoved down his throat—is becoming more and more common. All over the country, fathers of all races, creeds, and economic circumstances are confronting the mommy bias head-on. They are convincing judges that divorced dads deserve a break.

Several states now penalize custodial parents for blocking or refusing visitation time to the noncustodial parent, including California, New York, Illinois, New Jersey, and others. This turning tide is most evident in the rapid rise of a new approach to custody in which both parents are equal partners. It's called joint physical custody.

Sharing the Wealth

Joint physical custody, by which a child legally lives with both parents, is a growing—and well-documented—phenomenon. The Los Angeles–based Joint Custody Association responds to requests for information with a two hundred-page package of clippings, newsletters, and other pro joint-family armament.

Joint custody is also called shared parenting, but the two are not the same. Researchers will tell you that shared parenting refers to a type of postdivorce cooperation in which the less involved parent is with the child one-third of the time or more. Joint physical custody is a legal decree that awards responsibility for the children, including where they live as well as legal guardianship, to both parents equally.

The idea of splitting custody between Dad and Mom formally began in 1980 when California declared shared custody to be the "presumption" under which judges were to make decisions in divorce cases when children were involved. This meant that the court was to presume both parents would share physical custody unless a compelling case for another arrangement could be made.

It was a historic change: the first time any state formally repudiated the Tender Years Doctrine and refused to presume that one parent—virtually always the mother—should be awarded sole physical custody. Later the Golden State softened its bold stance somewhat in favor of a "no presumption" law, although the revised guidelines still strive to guarantee the children of divorce frequent contact with both parents. In fact, California courts are instructed to grant custody to whichever parent more facilitates contact with the other parent. Overall, the presumption of joint custody, through statutes or actual laws, is on the books in 80 percent of the states, and in fourteen of them, including Florida, Louisiana, and Texas, shared custody is the "preferred" custody solution.

There is no preferred formula, however. You start with a fifty-fifty split, say fathers with joint physical custody, and then, as one dad puts it, "you kind of vamp from there." There are as many types of joint custody arrangements as there are joint custody parents. Indeed, divorced dads who share physical custody of their children report that the arrangement is entirely fluid, changing as circumstances change. In these situations the children never spend exactly half their time with one parent and half with the other.

There are many critics of joint custody in the nation's courts. Feminists suspect that splitting custody is often a ploy by noncustodial dads to avoid paying child support. Some psychologists claim that a child's need for stability is unlikely to be met when the child bounces back and forth between two homes.

Despite its current popularity, joint custody is awarded in only a minority of all divorce settlements. Fewer than 20 percent of divorces involving children result in joint custody agreements. It is only possible when both parents give their consent, after all, and divorcing couples usually can't even agree on what time it is, let alone willingly share responsibility for their kids. Moreover, while American family law courts may recognize a child's need for both parents in principle, the allocation of custody in practice is still frequently influenced by lingering Tender Years attitudes. In many family law courts, it's tough for a dad to make a case for joint physical custody unless both he and his wife literally split parenting duties while married. The parent who was more often home taking care of the kids will usually keep them in the divorce, and that still means Mom most of the time.

When Arizona researcher Sanford Braver sifted through the results of his landmark study on divorce (it was a "landmark" simply because Braver talked to fathers as well as mothers), he was surprised by the gulf that separated the viewpoints of ex-spouses. They agreed on almost nothing, and their opinions were especially far apart on the subject of who should have physical custody of their kids.

In that regard, divorced parents have much in common with divorce experts. Nobody agrees on whether joint custody helps or hurts kids. Research, though, has consistently failed to show any direct link between joint custody and increased legal wrangling or, more importantly, maladjusted kids.

The Stanford Custody Project, which consisted of two studies of parents who filed for divorce in northern California between 1984 and 1985, found that kids in dual-resident or joint custody homes were very satisfied with the arrangement and were doing just fine three and a half years after their parents' separation. The custody arrangement itself was less important than the children's having a close relationship with the residential parent and not being caught between warring parents. The children of divorce who lived under the more conventional single-parent custody arrangement suffered no harm from being in close contact with the nonresidential parent (the father most of the time, of course) and were helped by such contact in at least some of the cases, especially when the children were adolescents. And when asked why they visited their nonresident parent, 88 percent of the adolescents interviewed in a follow-up study a year after the first one was conducted both the study researched all kinds of divorced homes said they wanted to do so.

Just Between You Two

Divorce is never easy, and it's usually made harder—and more expensive—when it's handled strictly by attorneys. The Children's Rights Council estimates that attorneys take in, at a minimum, about $1.5 billion in fees from divorce cases every year, but the actual figure is likely much higher. Most divorced dads pay at least $2,500 to get divorced without a trial, often double that, and that's just for *their* own lawyers— half of divorcing men pay for their wives' attorneys as well. The tab is far, far greater when men are forced to fight for custody. In fact, it's not uncommon for a litigant in a custody battle to shell out five or six figures to divorce lawyers. A big-city custody fight, in fact, will often rack up as much as $150,000 in legal bills.

Attorneys, by training, are used to operating in adversarial situations, so that's how they approach divorce and custody issues. But there's an alternative to family law court: it's called mediation. Mediation first appeared on the American divorce scene more or less at the same time as the fathers' rights movement. About half of the country's mediators are lawyers and half are social workers. They're court-appointed or privately hired counselors who work with divorcing couples to craft a mutually satisfactory settlement agreement in lieu of going to court.

Over the past two decades, mediation has built up momentum like a snowball down a mountainside. Today the practice is widespread, and some states require divorcing couples to attend at least one mediating session. In 1981 the Academy of Family Mediators was founded to train mediators and now boasts almost three thousand members around the world.

Although court systems increasingly refer divorcing couples to mediators, many couples seek out professional mediation on their own. Even after a divorce is settled, some couples continue to work with a mediator on such issues as parent-child relationships or visitation reassessment. Once a mediated agreement is filed with the court, it has the force of law.

In the beginning of the mediation boom, the nation's lawyers were typically loath to endorse a practice that deprived their clients of "winning" a custody battle. By the middle of the last decade, however, even the American Bar Association officially became pro-mediation. Social workers and psychologists, more inclined to think in terms of cooperative solutions by training, have always been strong advocates of the practice. Mediators must be trained to practice, and in many states, such as Virginia, they also must be court-certified.

The research on mediation is—surprise!—ambivalent about its overall benefits. There is widespread agreement, however, that mediation helps the children of divorce, since its goal is to decrease the amount of conflict between parents. It is certainly much cheaper than going to court: a 1990 study found that couples who went through traditional divorce court procedures spent 134 percent more than couples who mediated the dissolution of their marriage.

A Long Way to Come, a Long Way to Go

Recently, much media attention was focused on a deadbeat father who was caught and jailed for owing hundreds of thousands of dollars in back child support. It was a popular story, because deadbeat dads are popular villains in contemporary America. But one wonders why there isn't similar condemnation of custodial mothers who deny their exhusbands visitation, which affects the children of divorce just as dramatically.

The war on deadbeat dads is very public and quite sensational, but too often it is used as a pretext for attacking all divorced fathers. The truth is that deadbeat dads are the exception, not the rule.

According to government figures, fewer than half of the

nation's custodial parents (5.3 million, or 46 percent) were supposed to receive child support payments in 1991. More than 5 million custodial parents (divorced and never married) were without awards of financial support from their children's other parent. Two common reasons that these parents did not receive support payments were that they did not want an award or that the noncustodial parent was unable to pay.

About 6.9 million of the total 11.5 million noncustodial parents in the United States, mostly dads, had joint custody and/or visitation privileges to contact their children. These parents were far more likely to have made payments if they had one or both of those privileges than if they had neither, 79 percent versus 56 percent.

Yet anti-father support legislation, cloaked in righteous indignation, continues to be written into law. In 1992, for example, California raised many divorced dads' payments by as much as three times their original amount. So onerous was this Tender Years attack on male parenting that second wives got into the activist act, launching an organization called Coalition of Parent Support.

So the uncivil war is no longer completely one-sided, but unfortunately it is far from over. Consider how little has changed in the years since the 1979 hit film *Kramer vs. Kramer*, which did much to popularize the fathers' rights movement (and earned Dustin Hoffman an Oscar), and the 1994 hit movie *Mrs. Doubtfire*, starring Robin Williams in the heroic divorced dad role.

In *Kramer vs. Kramer*, New York City dad Hoffman is making a good life for his young son when he is dragged into a custody battle by his ex-wife, a wandering iconoclast who deserted her family. At the end, however, Mom has a miraculous and instantaneous change of heart, realizes that Dad is the better parent, and graciously gives up her claim to her son.

But not until after she wins sole custody in court.

In *Mrs. Doubtfire*, San Francisco dad Williams is forced to go to absurd lengths to remain a part of his children's lives (by creating his nanny persona, Mrs. Doubtfire), for which a judge pronounces him crazy and reduces his visitation privileges to brief, supervised encounters with his three kids in their mother's home. At the end, however, Mom has a miraculous and instantaneous change of heart, realizes that the creation of Dad's alter ego was an act of extraordinary parental love (not to mention very convenient for her as a working mom), and graciously agrees to let her ex-husband baby-sit the kids every afternoon.

But she still keeps sole custody.

Many of the dads I interviewed for this book had custody horror stories of their own to tell. Following are a few of those (courtesy of the Children's Rights Council).

Steve Nagy was a decorated war hero, held four university degrees, had been honored by his local Rotary and Kiwanis clubs, and served on the board of directors for an inner-city parochial school. He'd never been in trouble with the law, never even had a speeding ticket. Nagy had been a responsible husband for twenty-three years and had a strong, loving relationship with his ten-year-old son, Chip. But none of that mattered when his wife filed for divorce.

The judge in their New Jersey court denied Nagy the opportunity to present expert witnesses to rebut his ex-wife's charges (among them, that he was a drug addict and alcoholic and probably psychotic), threatened him with jail if he didn't use the real estate broker the judge recommended to sell the Nagys' house, and awarded Nagy's ex-wife sole physical custody of their son.

In Vermont, Bob Bancroft faced the specter of unbalanced scales when his ex-wife, with whom he had been sharing physical custody of their two young sons, requested sole custody. The court appointed a psychologist, who examined the parents and recommended joint physical custody. But the parents couldn't agree, and without that agreement, the Bancroft family's future was decided by a judge. Bancroft's wife was granted sole custody, and Bob was ordered to pay 55 percent of total child support costs.

In Georgia, Jim Wagner had custody of his four children for ten years, and for eight of those years received no child support from his ex-wife, who worked outside the home. When two of the four children elected to live with their mother, the court waived her arrears payments, ordered Jim to pay support for the two who were with their mother, and removed her from any support obligation for the two living with him, even though she and Jim earned comparable salaries.

Jim filed a motion to set aside the order. The court responded by taking the other two children away from him and ordering him to pay $6,000 of his ex-wife's legal fees. When he could not pay within fifteen days, Wagner was thrown into jail.

Many fathers are forced to fight for their kids even when they don't contest maternal custody. Visitation, probably a divorced dad's most basic right, can be and often is threatened. Often the interference a father experiences takes the form of an ongoing, taunting kind of activity, like never having the children ready on time when Dad comes to pick them up. This is difficult to prove in court, because it's so subtle.

For most of the past century, when a divorced dad who was denied access decided to fight, he found himself at the mercy of a system stacked against him. And the options available to him were both limited and unappealing. A father could file for a change in custody status, but that inflamed what by definition was already an incendiary relationship between the divorced parents, and was a hard battle to win, as we've seen. Plus judges have always been reluctant to change an existing postdivorce setup. A dad being denied visitation could argue that his ex-wife was in contempt of the court's divorce decree and try to have the mother jailed, but that was hardly a recipe for a healthy postdivorce family environment.

Sometimes the battle was lost before a father even got to the courtroom. Lawyers, like everyone else in our society, were taught that maternal sole custody was the legal path of least resistance. Divorcing fathers were often counseled by their own lawyers to avoid a court fight over custody because the father's chances were usually so slim. During his divorce, Steve Nagy interviewed eleven different attorneys. Every one of them told him not to even bother fighting for custody of his son because a male didn't stand a chance in the New Jersey divorce courts.

Michigan's system provides a typical example of how custody is determined. Judges presiding over custody cases there are asked to make their determinations based on the "best interests of the child," which, under the state's Child Custody Act, is divined from consideration of the following twelve factors. Note the emphasis on Tender Years code words like "continuity" and "stability." Still, the Michigan dozen can serve as rules of thumb for divorced dads to use in gauging their own parenting position in the eyes of the law. Custody in Michigan is awarded based on:

1. The love, affection and other emotional ties existing between the parties involved and the child;
2. The capacity and disposition of the parties involved to give the child love, affection, guidance and continuation of the educating and raising of the child in the child's religion or creed, if any;
3. The capacity and disposition of the parties involved to provide the child with food, clothing, medical care or other remedial care recognized and permitted under the laws of [Michigan] in place of medical care, and other material needs;

4. The length of time the child has lived in a stable, satisfactory environment, and the desirability of maintaining continuity;
5. The permanence, as a family unit, of the existing or proposed custodial home or homes;
6. The moral fitness of the parties involved;
7. The mental and physical health of the parties involved;
8. The home, school, and community record of the child;
9. The reasonable preference of the child, if the court deems the child to be of sufficient age to express preference;
10. The willingness and ability of each of the parents to facilitate and encourage close and continuing parent-child relationships between the child and the other parent;
11. Domestic violence, regardless of whether the violence was directed against or witnessed by the child;
12. Any other factor considered by the court to be relevant to the particular child custody dispute.

When It Comes to Custody, Time Is of the Essence

When our son was six years old, my ex-wife and I agreed to take him to see a child psychologist. Alex had been involved in several incidents of fighting and disobedience at summer camp that appeared to us to be more serious than typical little-boy misbehavior. We were worried that he was suffering from the aftereffects of our divorce.

After a few months of seeing the therapist, Alex was doing a lot better, and the shrink concluded that we could end the sessions. He told us our son had a few divorce-related "issues," but in general he was a healthy, happy kid, if a bit boisterous. The good doctor thanked us for working together for Alex's benefit and said it was rare to see two divorced people cooperate so effectively.

"If you were the mean of divorced couples," the therapist said to us, "my job would be a lot easier."

Livia and I beamed with pride at this, although we were a little nonplussed by the compliment. We don't think we're any better at child-rearing than most other divorced couples with kids. Like everybody else in our position, we have trouble even tolerating each other sometimes, let alone working together toward a common goal. But one thing we do agree on is that I should spend as much time as possible with Alex.

Livia doesn't play games with access, either by denying me agreed-upon visitation or by blocking me from spending time with Alex beyond what our settlement specifies. So I have enough time not only to do the dad things I'm reasonably good at, but, more important, to learn from my inevitable fathering mistakes and correct them.

If there's one thing I know now that I wish I knew when we were negotiating my divorce, it's that quantity is as important as quality in fathering. I really thought, and I think most men still believe, that what you do with your kids is more important than how long you have to do it. But that's not true.

The family experts understand this. Their definition of shared parenting, formal or informal, is based on time spent with the kids. Period. Not what parents do with the kids, but how much time they spend with them. If either parent does not have the child at least one-third of the time, it's not shared parenting.

I did not seek time guarantees in our settlement when we were getting divorced. Most of the time I spend with Alex is not specifically mandated by our settlement. This includes arrangements that have been in effect in our nonnuclear family for years, such as having Alex sleep over every Thursday night instead of just having dinner with me. So every time my ex and I fight, which still happens a few times a year even in a relatively "civilized" divorce like mine, I worry about being denied access. I have never been blocked from seeing my boy, of course, but that's just the luck of the draw: I've got a reasonable ex-spouse. The point is, I'm vulnerable because I don't have any legally protected guarantees.

If you are in the midst of divorcing, remember that how much time you negotiate with your children is just as critical as what you do with the time you get. (In later chapters, we will discuss how to make time for yourself and your kids without the benefit of specific agreements.)

Joint physical custody, of course, is your best guarantee of enough time with your kids. The odds of your winning joint physical custody, however, depend on many variables beyond your direct control, such as the prevailing attitude of family courts in your county or state, the kind of judge you get, the competence of the respective attorneys in your divorce, the influence of feminist and/or family values activists in your area, and so forth. Bottom line, joint physical custody is awarded in only a small minority of custody cases in the United States.

Conventional noncustodial arrangements, the likely starting point for most divorcing fathers, only give dads access to their kids about 20 percent of the time, which is not nearly enough. If you aren't going to get joint physical custody, you're going to have to do some settlement sculpting. Here are five "time keepers" you can use to make sure your divorce settlement gives you enough time for fatherhood.

Divorced-Dad Time Keepers

"Legalize" your involvement. Joint legal custody is awarded to many fathers, but on the surface that's just a nice way to reassure dads that they still matter. The designation doesn't provide for any specific access or visitation privileges. It can be a powerful tool for you to protect your dad-dom, however, because joint legal custody means you legally share re-

sponsibility for your child's education and health with your ex-wife. Demand joint legal custody and be sure the agreement spells out in writing when and how often you take the child to the dentist or to the doctor, and that you also will be present at parents' night so your kid can show you the caterpillar model he made. Each of these typical parenting tasks provide you time with your child that is not automatically included in the usual court-mandated, noncustodial parent arrangement.

Secure "time chunks." Giving divorced dads their kids for a week or two every summer is axiomatic in our country; it's almost an American tradition. Therefore, most ex-wives won't have trouble with the concept of letting the kids live with you for a fortnight. Take advantage of this. Even if you live down the street, try to accumulate as many time "chunks" in your settlement as possible. In addition to the hot-weather season, some dads negotiate a week at Christmastime, or during spring break. Once again, if this is a formal part of your agreement, it can't be taken away from you on a whim or in anger.

Stack up holiday time. Custody agreements typically alternate visitation between divorcing spouses on major holidays (Christmas, Memorial Day, Easter, Labor Day, Thanksgiving, the Fourth of July, sometimes New Year's Eve and New Year's Day). Dad also usually gets the kids on his birthday and Father's Day. But those aren't the only times you celebrate during the year. Try to work in a few more opportunities to be with your kids—their paternal grandparents' birthdays or anniversary, for example; other religious holidays; Presidents' Day; Earth Day; Arbor Day. The list is endless. How about Halloween? Dads always forget to demand at least alternate visitation on All Hallow's Eve—arguably the celebration with the most child-parent bonding opportunities of any holiday besides Christmas.

Baby-sit. This one is short and sweet. Make it official that you have the right of first refusal to baby-sit your kid.

Include a "policy statement." One divorced dad decided to give himself blanket protection against access denial, a simple but wonderfully effective idea that has blessed this good man with the kind of peace of mind the rest of us divorced dads can only envy. "When we drew up our divorce agreement," the dad explains, "it was eight pages long. Seven and a half pages were what she wanted. The last half-page included a paragraph that says I have unlimited and unrestricted visitation rights. That's all I wanted. And I've never had a problem seeing my son whenever I want to."

Every divorcing father should demand a similar paragraph in his divorce agreement. I sure wish I had one in mine.

We've talked about the parents, the courts, and the issues. In the next chapter, we'll talk about the kids and how they feel about and react to divorce.

CHAPTER 2

---◆---

Sacrificial Lambs:
The Children of Divorce

What's done to children, they will do to society.

—Karl Menninger

A recent *Doonesbury* comic strip by Garry Trudeau showed a young girl, maybe ten years old, walking through a wintry forest with her divorced dad.

Concerned about her mother's lifestyle, the girl asks, "Poppy, don't you think ol' Momster has made a big mess of her life?"

"Sweeter," answers her father, "even if I thought so, I'd never tell you."

"Why not?"

"Because divorce is rough enough on a kid without parents tearing each other down."

"Wow ... that's pretty big of you, Daddy." She thinks

about this for a minute, then turns to her father. "I don't have to be that big, do I?"

"Heck, no, you're the victim," says Dad. "Go nuts."

Most published estimates put the number of children of divorce in this country at 18 million. One million children endure the breakup of their parents' marriage every year, and that figure has remained constant for at least the past two decades. Moreover, since about 40 percent of all U.S. marriages still end in divorce, it's safe to assume those ranks will continue to grow.

Divorce can devastate even the strongest men and women, and it may be even tougher on their children, who, like their parents, think of the end of their family as a tremendous personal failure. More to the point, divorce can affect a child longer and more profoundly than it does the divorcing parents themselves. And yet, believe it or not, with some youngsters the effect is surprisingly positive.

Kids from divorced families are forced to grow up faster than other kids, which sometimes makes them smarter and wiser. Reality intrudes on their childhood rudely, often brutally, and they must adapt. Like their parents, these children react to the challenge of divorce in an infinite variety of ways. The key to how well kids ultimately fare after divorce, though, is how their parents relate to them.

Finding the Silver Lining

Karen was in the first grade when her parents divorced. She enjoyed a strong relationship with her custodial mother and her noncustodial father, and grew up to be a happy, well-adjusted young woman. That's why Karen's mom was a bit startled when her daughter reached her late teens and suddenly began asking questions about what really happened during her parents' divorce.

Karen's mother answered the questions as objectively as

she could. Then she asked her daughter, "Do you ever regret that your father and I got divorced?"

Karen looked at her mom and giggled. "The way you two got along, I'm surprised I was ever conceived in the first place."

Think about the children of divorce that you know. (In modern America, everybody knows at least one or two of them.) Chances are they're pretty much like Karen. Most are probably dealing with issues caused by their parents' divorce, although some may be more obvious about it than others, but in the main they're good kids. They don't get pregnant. They don't join gangs. They don't pack heat in elementary school. Most of them steer clear of drugs.

Why? Where are all the fallen youth the doomsday experts apparently trip over every time they leave their homes? I'll tell you where they are: anywhere there are uncaring, dysfunctional, or physically and emotionally absent parents. It doesn't matter if these lost boys and girls are black or white, upper-class or below the poverty line. It doesn't make a bit of difference if their parents are still married or not, or even if they ever were married. What makes a family healthy is the kind of parenting that goes on within it, not its legal status or whether everybody sleeps under the same roof every night.

Yes, your child will have difficulty dealing with the emotional tidal wave that accompanies divorce. Didn't you? To be sure, your kid faces challenges that kids who live in nuclear families don't have to address. Do your married friends wrestle with the same issues of loss, guilt, anger, and failure that you do? Sad to say, some children of divorce remain scarred psychologically by their parents' breakup long after the divorce, maybe even their whole lives—it's true, for example, that kids from sundered families seem to have a greater need for love and reassurance than children who have grown up in intact families. But how secure are you about the ability of your relationships to endure?

Some days are better than others, right? But, in general,

you turned out okay. You're not on top of a tower with a rifle, or desperately trying to score crack in the bad part of town at three in the morning. Divorce was a tough test for you, probably the toughest you've ever had to face, but you survived. You may even be prospering.

Likewise, none of the special problems related to divorce that your kids will be forced to deal with will sentence them to a lifetime of misery. Divorce does not inevitably ruin people's lives. In fact, most of us, dads and kids, do just fine. Even the gloomiest research reveals that the majority of kids with divorced parents grow up happy and well-adjusted.

You wouldn't know it by reading the coverage such studies receive, though. When the effects of divorce on children are explored, attention focuses almost exclusively on the bad things that happen when parents divorce, not on the success stories.

As a journalist, I can attest to the fact that something negative is always more newsworthy than something positive, whether it's world affairs, local news, sports scores, or a feature on divorce. A story warning that disaster looms right around the corner will make the front page, but one reporting that the sky is not falling will merit merely a paragraph at the back of the paper, right above the discount tire ads. So the studies that get the headlines paint the bleakest picture of postdivorce life and dismiss what goes right with faint qualifiers. Those are the studies reporters write about, that's the angle divorce researchers take when they present their findings, and any evidence to the contrary is downplayed or ignored.

A famous axiom attributed to David Ogilvy, one of the great legends of American advertising, is that research is too often used the way a drunk uses a lamppost: for support rather than illumination. If you go looking for the ravages of divorce on children, you will undoubtedly find them, but you can just as quickly find examples where divorce didn't destroy a family, or, conversely, where children in intact families were psychologically damaged by dysfunction.

Speaking of dysfunctional nuclear families, they can be quite destructive. Philadelphia family counselor Gwen Olitsky, who teaches future therapists at the Self-Help Institute for Training and Therapy, tells the story of a student, unconvinced that there were no good reasons to break up a marriage, who declared that no one in his family had ever gotten divorced. Olitsky asked him, "Well, then how did those family members divorce themselves from each other?"

The student just looked at her in confusion, but everyone else in the class smiled and nodded. With a little more prodding, he admitted that although few overt arguments took place in his family, subversive divorce-type conflict occurred with regularity. Between his parents, for example, most of the dysfunctional communication was delivered via innuendo or gesture, and there was frequent verbal taunting and belittling.

Suddenly the student understood: a marriage can break up without the parents physically separating. And this young man faced the same emotional problems as those faced by children of divorce.

A bad intact marriage was the American family ubervillain not so long ago. Remember being peppered with stories about how awful it was to grow up in a stunted emotional family? Remember how everything that went wrong with your job or your lovers or your relationship with your dog was somehow your parents' fault? Remember when dysfunctional families spelled the death knell of civilization? Now it's divorce's turn to wear the black hat.

Just the Facts? Not Always

Not surprisingly, research into the state of the American family often comes up with misleading results because the subjects of these studies are not representative of all divorced families. In fact, until recently the Census Bureau never even bothered to query fathers.

Arizona researcher Sanford Braver delivers the definitive criticism of this one-sided approach to divorce research. "Anybody who has had much contact with divorced parents in any numbers realizes that, in general, they don't like each other much," he says. "So if you talk to only one of them, whichever one you talk to, you will get your story colored to only one point of view."

Indeed, you don't have to prod a researcher very hard to elicit the admission that almost anybody can make numbers appear to prove anything. And sometimes the results of a particular study are used to prove or disprove the same claim. To my mind, the best example of the vulnerability of research findings to abuse by partisans of one side or another is found in the work of famous divorce researcher/psychotherapist Dr. Judith Wallerstein. In her seminal 1970s study, the California Children of Divorce Project, Wallerstein and her partner, Joan Kelly, found 37 percent of the young subjects in their study doing badly five years after their parent's divorce. But the finding also shows, of course, that the majority of these kids—more than six out of ten—were doing fine. Yet the study is trumpeted today as unarguable evidence that divorce dooms a child to a life of crime or worse.

When Wallerstein and Kelly probed for the reasons behind the continued problems of the unfortunate minority, it's not at all surprising that they found, for the most part, that the kids' parents were still feuding, often bitterly—further evidence that the degree of conflict between ex-spouses has far more impact on children than marital status per se.

In 1980 Wallerstein's book *Surviving the Breakup* was embraced by advocates of joint physical custody as proof of the efficacy of shared parenting. But her outlook appeared to become progressively bleaker as the decade progressed. In one of her latest books, *Second Chances*, Wallerstein explored the adjustment of divorced families a decade after their breakup. At the very end of the paperback version of the book, readers are told that the intent of *Second Chances* was "not to argue against divorce but rather to raise the consciousness of the community about the long-term effects of divorce on children."

But other divorce experts have countered that what you won't read in the book is how what happens to kids from divorced families compares to what happens to kids whose parents have rotten marriages. These critics note that half the parents in the *Second Chances* study were described as having moderate to severe psychological problems. More to the point for us divorced parents, the book offers no concrete recommendations about how to help kids avoid divorce-related problems or handle them when they do arise.

Wallerstein, in any case, has drawn considerable criticism from her own colleagues. Even her former partner Joan Kelly is uncomfortable with Wallerstein's profoundly pessimistic viewpoint. Plus, Wallerstein's critics contend that her lack of control groups leaves her open to rebuttal.

What divorced dads should focus on when they ponder the task ahead of them is that there are two sides to every story. People have forgotten yesterday's doomsday headlines about the bad things that can happen when warring parents don't divorce. And as I stated in the foreword, those of us who decided to end our marriages didn't get divorced casually. We didn't get up one day and say to ourselves, "You know, I'm kinda bored being a husband." We got divorced for good reason, often because staying married would be worse for our kids than breaking up. We know we made the right decision.

And sooner or later, so do our kids.

After the Fall: You're Not the Only One Who's Angry

It would seem axiomatic that children sometimes react badly to the divorce of their parents, but parents waste an unbelievable amount of time trying to figure out if their kids' bad or erratic behavior is or isn't directly related to the divorce rather than doing something about the behavior. Of course it's related.

Your kids are going through whatever you're going through, but because they're kids, their ability to understand what's happening to them is less developed. Consequently, their responses aren't necessarily going to be directly traceable to the breakup of your marriage. The trauma of your divorce probably caused you to engage in some bad or just plain pathetic behavior. Did you run around with women half your age? Drink too much? Or did you go the other way and become a "work monk," submerging your anger, grief, and sense of failure in your job? Whatever your particular story, you probably did something in that first year or two after your divorce that in hindsight seems foolish or silly or just plain self-destructive. So don't be surprised when your children do similiarly silly or self-destructive things.

If they're still tykes when you and your wife part, they may become preoccupied with minutiae. Who is going to take them to Little League practice? What if they forget their toothbrush at their house when they go visit Daddy? Just keep reassuring them, answering their questions calmly. You can do wonders for a divorced kid's insecurities just by appearing to be in control of the situation. (For other tips on making kids feel better in these situations, see Chapter Five.)

Or your kid may become mired in hypothetical musings. "Daddy, if Mommy moves to New York, will I still see you?" "Daddy, what if you get another job?" These are disaster scenarios to a child whose world has already been blown to bits. Again, *calm reassurance in a steady voice and straight answers at the level of the child's understanding will offer comfort.*

Your kids may respond to your divorce by becoming extremely possessive, even selfish, of their time with you. They become master manipulators. They may act "bad" because it keeps you involved with their lives. These reactions don't mean you have budding monsters on your hands, however.

Kids, it turns out, are actually more likely to "act out" than their parents are. (For some reason no one has yet been able to fathom, boys are hit harder by divorce than girls. It may be related to their relatively greater need for authority figures and the fact that their same-sex parent is probably the absent one.) Nothing short of the death of a parent is as traumatic to a child as divorce. The bad news is that divorce does increase the odds that your children will have emotional problems: they'll be angry, they'll be destructive, they'll be hard to discipline.

Of course, you know that. But knowing it and doing something about it are not always the same thing. The effects of divorce on kids are not always blindingly obvious; there may be subtle personality changes you simply don't notice. And most of your allies in child-rearing—educators, pediatricians, child psychologists, camp counselors—are going to tiptoe around any assumption about how your kids are reacting to your divorce. They'll hem and haw and qualify their observations.

You are the one who has to make the right determination and the tough decisions.

The good news is, while the pain of divorce may never leave, its intensity usually subsides eventually. Studies indicate that children whose behavior declines after divorce often bounce back to their predivorce behavior after two years (the standard period of postdivorce adjustment when most of the open conflict between parents occurs). A general rule of thumb is that your kids are going to be as angry as you and your ex-wife are. If there's a high degree of hostility between you and their mom, chances are good they'll demonstrate a high degree of hostility as well, which may take any number of forms of disobedience or troublemaking.

The National Institute of Child Health and Human Development charted the behavior of boys in intact homes and in homes where the parents were divorced or separated, over a two-year period. It found that the behavior of boys whose parents split during the study period was considerably more likely to worsen—35 percent compared to 19 percent for boys in intact homes. Still, just under half (48 percent) of the divorced-family kids in the study showed no change in behavior, and in 18 percent of the families, the boys' behavior actually improved (probably because the split reduced or eliminated the children's exposure to warring parents). The pattern was similar for girls.

One behavior you may have already faced with your child is the "let's play Dad off against Mom" maneuver, and vice versa. I think it's a universal reflex of kids to try and manipulate adults, but in divorce it's almost a survival instinct.

"Mommy lets me." "I'm going to ask Daddy." Don't fall for it. Your kids are children of the nineties. They know enough about divorce to think this ploy can help them get what they want. And since divorce is the ultimate lack of control for a kid, they may feel compelled to do what they can to regain control. Playing you off against your ex is a way for the kids to feel, however inaccurately, that they have some power over what is happening to their family. Stay the course, and usually your kids will outgrow it as they become acclimated to their new postdivorce life.

Until the Shaking Stops: The Emotional Aftermath

A sort of death occurs when two people divorce: the demise of a nuclear family. And, just as when loved ones pass on, the survivors of a deceased union need time to mourn. As we've noted, most experts use two years as a rough yardstick for how long it takes to go through this mourning period and "recover" from a divorce. The truth is, however, your now-sundered family will always go through peaks and valleys where things improve, worsen, then improve again. Often the reasons for a regression in your children's behavior can be surprising.

After they'd been apart for two and a half years, things between Kevin and his ex-wife were finally beginning to settle down. But for some reason life was becoming harder for Kevin's two little daughters. One day both girls came home from school in tears because the other kids told them they didn't have a full-time Mommy and Daddy. The crying perplexed their parents, because the girls had handled much rougher teasing before without any problem.

It took a period of soul-searching and gentle parental questioning, but Kevin finally figured out that the relative peace between him and his ex was depriving the girls of a post-divorce necessity: constant communication. "Because things were getting better, we were slipping into a different routine," he recalls. "Early in the divorce, we would make sure that the girls were able to talk about everything. Once things settled down, neither of us was spending as much time discussing issues with the kids."

Schoolyard tormentors aside, most of the problems your kids will wrestle with probably will have to do with internal rather than external demons. After all, the children's entire universe is shattered when their parents divorce. Children react the way anybody would if the things they loved and depended on were suddenly and violently snatched away. They become sad, angry, and especially guilty—whether the guilt is expressed verbally or not, your children are almost certainly going to blame themselves to some degree for the divorce.

No matter what their ages, you must constantly reassure your children that you didn't leave because of them. The divorce is not their fault. If they've very young, explain that Mommy isn't leaving. Tell them Mommy and Daddy aren't always nice to each other when they're together, that happens sometimes, and it's better for everybody if they don't live together. But assure them that you will always be there for them. If your kids are older, of course, you don't have to use baby talk. But they're still going to need reassurance from you, and they will continue to need it forever. Don't ever stop giving it.

Your kids will not jump onto the table and shout, "It's my fault!" or "I'm in distress!" But they'll give you clues: acting as if they can't do anything right, calling themselves "bad" or "stupid."

If you argue with your ex over a parenting issue, for example, your child may try to accept blame for the argument, even going so far as to dispute with you who was to blame. Your child also might mirror your emotional state. If you're calmly trying to explain why you blew up at her mom, your daughter might say, just as calmly, that she could have done something differently to avoid the resultant contretemps.

Preschoolers may think the divorce is punishment for a bad thought, or that Daddy is leaving because they are bad or unlovable. Kids aged three to five are in constant fear of abandonment when their parents divorce, and they may be thinking that if you left, Mom could go any day now. Very young children may not articulate this fear directly, but they'll manifest it in behavior calculated to keep you around. They'll regress. If they're in the middle of potty training, for example, they may suddenly start having trouble. Every time there's an "accident," Mommy and Daddy come together to discuss the best way of dealing with the problem.

Teenagers, surprisingly, often have the most severe problems with guilt following their parents' divorce, figuring that their typically adolescent obstinacy or surliness or both somehow caused the breakup.

Of particular concern to divorced parents is how their divorce will affect their children's attitudes toward marriage. It's a valid concern. The children of divorce manifest a relatively greater need to be loved than other kids do, not necessarily in a dramatic way, but as a kind of quiet quest. Depending on how well their parents get along, such children may also regard relationships or the institution of marriage with great skepticism.

George Handley, the therapist who specializes in divorced men clients, admits that his oldest son, now in his early twenties, is extremely suspicious of the very idea of marriage. The young man has never had a long-term relationship, by choice.

Another child of divorce, Martin, whose parents first separated when he was in fifth grade, believes that "love hurts
a lot." But he's learned from his parents' mistakes as well.
Each of his parents tried to change the other. That approach
obviously didn't work. So Martin learned to accept his girlfriends for who they are, not what he might imagine they
should be. A valuable life lesson learned *because* his parents
divorced, not in spite of it. And recently Martin became engaged to a wonderful girl.

Therein lies the moral of this section. Just as you don't have
to accept antisocial behavior from your children as an inevitable consequence of your divorce, you need not resign yourself that they will be unlucky in love and generally have a
miserable time of it in relationships.

Clearly, your parental work in this regard will be more
difficult than it is for parents in intact families. Honesty and
communication are the keys. Your children will wrestle with
questions of inevitability, and you must reassure them that
not all relationships are bad and they don't all break up.
Teach your kid that everybody is entitled to a healthy and
loving relationship. More important, everybody can find one.
And a little mea culpa isn't bad at all; once they reach the
age of seven or so, your kids can absorb intangible ideas,
including the truly astounding one that their parents are human . . . and make mistakes.

The Times of Their Lives: Divorce Reactions by Age

Of all the wonders his fourteen-month-old daughter shows
Minneapolis single dad Rhoeshon Dillard every weekend
when she stays with him, perhaps the most awe-inspiring is
her ability to intuit what he means without understanding
what he's saying. "We can feel each other," he says. "She'll
go to grab something, I'll say her name, and she'll look at me
and put it down. Somehow, she knows what's up. It's
weird."

But it isn't really. Rhoeshon's tender observation, as I'm sure parents with infants and toddlers will agree, is universal. Children in the first year or so of life are preverbal, which means they pick up on emotional states. They may not remember their parents fighting in front of them, for example, but they sure know something bad is happening.

This is a critical must-do for a divorced dad: *Know what to expect from your children at their age level.* Children react differently to divorce at different ages. This maxim may seem obvious, but common sense is in very short supply during and right after a divorce, and many parents aren't thinking straight. You'd be surprised how much this age level awareness can help ease the problems for your child.

An infant or toddler, for example, is attuned to what shrinks call "emotional resonance," a fancy phrase that simply means they don't know what you're saying, but they know what you're feeling and they feel it too. You may get into a juicy insult match with your ex because you don't think your eighteen-month-old understands what's going on, but believe me, she does.

A few years down the line and it's "the universe revolves around me" time. Preschoolers believe nothing happens in the world that they didn't make happen. For these kids, the usually farfetched concern that they'll be left parentless and defenseless or that Daddy will disappear forever if he walks out that door isn't figurative. They literally believe those things will happen.

By the time kids are six years old or a little older, they've formed some pretty strong attachments to the notion of family. It's a rock to them, a wall on which they can lean for support, a cushion full of love that they can depend on. Then, poof! It's gone. Imagine how that feels. This is the age when kids learn how to conceptualize. They start creating disaster scenarios, and divorce is a breeding ground for dark fantasies about what will happen next. You have to be alert with children this age, because they internalize like crazy. This is where the "I don't know" answers to questions about how they feel about the divorce can really drive you up a wall. But don't stop asking.

As they approach their teen years (ten to twelve), kids are able to understand what divorce really means, but their responses are still grounded in self-blame and anger. This is the stage, experts say, where they may start siding with one parent against the other. One warning sign that a child is having trouble is when a preadolescent child acts unemotionally about his parents' divorce. Another is sudden and mysterious medical problems, like headaches. We'll meet one of these kids, in fact, in a later chapter.

If this happens to your kids, try the indirect approach. Tell them, "Sometimes kids act angry when they're really scared of losing someone, and that's normal." Words to this effect often help start the healing process in an emotionally wounded preadolescent.

Teenagers, of course, need another emotional problem like they need a giant pimple on the tip of their nose. Divorce makes an especially miserable time of life utterly unendurable. Teens may be the neediest children of divorce, because they depend on their parents a lot more than most of them are likely to admit even to themselves. Mom and Dad splitting up is almost an insult to them. How could you, just when I need you most? This is why divorce precipitates so much rage in teenage children.

Neither adult nor child, a teenager lives in a perilous limbo that at best is uncomfortable and at worst deadly. For dads with teenagers (and even dads with younger kids, since your little ones will become teenagers all too soon) a new study of almost 300,000 teenagers by the Search Institute offers some guidelines.

The Institute asked 273,000 students in grades six through twelve in eight states to complete a 152-question survey and summarized the findings in a book called *What Kids Need to Succeed: Proven, Practical Ways to Raise Good Kids,* by Peter L. Benson, Judy Galbraith, and Pamela Espeland. According to the study, kids need thirty "assets" to succeed, divided into sixteen external assets and fourteen internal assets. Most kids in the study had sixteen of the assets, but that wasn't enough—the best adjusted kids were the ones with at least twenty of the assets and the worst were the ones with ten or fewer. Not surprisingly, having an adult or adults who really cared about them was especially important in how the teens in the study were doing.

External	Internal
Warm, caring family home	Desire to achieve
Approachable parents	Desire to advance educationally
Communicative parents	Desire for above-average grades
Other approachable adults	Self-discipline to do six or more hours of homework a week
Other communicative adults	Desire to help people
Parental involvement in school	Global concern
Positive school climate	Empathy
Parental standards	Sexual restraint
Parental discipline	Assertiveness skills
Parental monitoring	Friendship-making skills
Limits on away-from-home socializing	Planning skills
Positive peer influences	Self-esteem
Music lessons	Hope
Organized extracurricular activities	
Community activities	
Involvement with a faith community	

The Search Institute list is a good reference to use as you develop your divorced-dad parenting philosophy. And you will notice that none of the assets deals with marital status ("warm, caring family home" is not a euphemism for "nuclear family").

A Little Something for Everyone

The differences in children of divorce by age sound daunting enough if you have just one little infant when your marriage breaks up. Now realize that as time goes on, you're going to have to deal with all the stages in one way or another. Divorce isn't like the common cold; you don't get some rest, take a pill, call your doctor in the morning, and everything's jake again. It's a process that ebbs and flows for years.

Still, don't be glum. You can handle all this because the causes of the worst divorce effects are the same no matter what the children's ages, and hence so are their solutions.

The number one trigger for emotional problems in kids of all ages is—you guessed it—conflict between you and your ex-spouse. From the time you tell them about the divorce until the day after forever, the amount of hostility between you and your ex-wife is going to be mirrored in the problems your kids are having. This can't be emphasized enough: avoiding conflict with your ex is the one thing you can do that can literally make or break your postdivorce parenting strategy.

Another prime contributor to kids' problems no matter what their ages is parental neediness. Divorce takes a mighty chunk out of our self-image, and many parents, male and female, use their kids as shoulders to cry on or—just as bad—try to enlist them as allies in their war against the other parent. This is particularly prevalent with preadolescent and teen children. No matter at what stage it happens, it's a nasty habit that's going to hurt your kids more than it will help you.

The last piece in the puzzle of helping kids cope with divorce is restoring stability and continuity to their lives. As soon as possible and as completely as possible, create a postdivorce scheme with your ex that builds a new, day-to-day reliability. I go to Dad's on such-and-such days. Mommy drops me off and Daddy picks me up at school on those days. Wednesday nights are Father's Nights. And so on. Human beings crave dependability—little humans more than most.

Counsel for Their Defense: Getting Help for Kids

In 1990 the judicial system in Michigan's Oakland County launched a program called SMILE (Start Making It Livable for Everyone). The intent of this somewhat embarrassingly named group was simple: to help divorced parents with children under the age of eighteen remain good parents. SMILE was formed to give sundered nuclear families the tools they need to get over the pain of divorce, and most important, to ensure that the children of divorce keep both parents in their lives. (One of the tools they highly recommend is counseling.)

Today SMILE includes almost six thousand fathers and mothers and about ten thousand children. The program has blossomed to more than thirty counties across the state. I don't think the rapid success of the SMILE program is due solely to the local citizenry. I believe it addresses a gaping need in the postdivorce safety net: *Kids need counseling; make sure yours get it.*

Like divorce itself, therapy suffers from a stigma in this country. People tend to regard you as at least neurotic and possibly dangerously psychotic if you go to a shrink. Or they think of counseling as an extravagant waste of time and expense, a perk of the moneyed class. That's foolishness. Therapy is a tool for living in the modern world. We should all be grateful that we have the ability to handle the inner problems that drove our forefathers crazy. You go to a gym to work on your body and you go to a therapist to work on your psyche. No difference. And nobody has more stuff to work out than a child of divorce.

If you're like most divorced dads, you won't blanch at this

prospect. You'll take help wherever you can get it. If you're reluctant to get your kids some good counseling, overcome your reservations. Your kids will benefit. I don't know any child of divorce, at any age, who hasn't.

You can get referrals for therapists who specialize in the children of divorce from many places, including their pediatrician, self-help groups, schools, churches, and other divorced dads. You'll have to consider several criteria:

- *Accessibility.* A therapist shouldn't be too far away (you don't want to make it easy for anybody to bail on an appointment).
- *Experience.* The therapist should specialize in or at least have an affinity for talking to kids the same age and gender as your own.
- *Compatibility.* This is the most important criterion. If your kid doesn't like the shrink, find another one. It's a waste of time trying to force anyone to open up to somebody he doesn't like or trust.

Kid Care: Tips to Help You Help Your Children

Like so many men and women who become involved in children's rights, Michael Oddenino knows firsthand about American divorce. A prominent southern California divorce lawyer, Oddenino is also a divorced father (since remarried). He remembers the brief but enlightening moments that taught him how to be a better dad. Like the time he realized that fathers only looked their kids in the eye when they were mad at them. Or the time in the car when his daughter, exasperated that she couldn't get Mom and Dad's attention, hollered from the backseat, "Please, I need listening parents!"

From these and other experiences, Oddenino put together a book called *Putting Kids First*. The book is filled with useful tips, in particular Oddenino's five keys to good parenting. Because they were written by a man, the keys are particularly useful to fathers. Every one of us should memorize them and put them to use whenever we're with our kids.

1. *Unconditional love.* They're your kids no matter what.
2. *Loving physical contact.* Hug them a lot.
3. *Loving eye contact.* Look your kids in the eye when you're happy with them as well as when you're angry with them.
4. *Loving ear contact.* Don't always dictate the agenda of a conversation; listen to your kids as well as telling them what to do.
5. *Develop your own self-esteem.* In a divorce, everybody gets down on himself or herself, but don't try to compensate by competing with your ex-spouse for your children's love.

So don't despair when politicians rant about guys like you as if you were a serial killer because you're no longer married. Pay no attention to the books, magazines, and newspaper stories with the screaming headlines, to the bilious radio talk show hosts and sensational TV shows that portray your kids as future gangbangers because you got divorced. Your children will not grow up fatally flawed if you do three things:

1. *Love* your kids no matter what.
2. *Be there* whenever they need you.
3. *Recognize and address* the common emotional problems children of divorce face.

Forever Questions

Fourteen-year-old Jim's parents separated when he was two and a half and divorced when he was four. His mom had custody of him, and he lived with her in New Jersey. His dad soon moved to Hawaii, and Jim flies out there for six weeks during the summer and a couple of weeks during Christmas vacation.

When he was in the second grade, Jim's parents waged an ugly and vicious four-month custody battle. He lived with his paternal grandparents during that time by court decree. The judge ultimately ruled in his mother's favor, and she retained custody.

Jim's father is distant in spirit as well as in body, and although his mother is devoted to him, she has had numerous personal problems. Nevertheless, this young man is lively, intelligent, extremely well-adjusted, and confident. That's a major reason he was asked to take part in a Banana Splits discussion group at school when he was in the seventh grade. Banana Splits is a program for children of divorce in which kids meet in groups of five or six once or twice a month during the school year to talk about their lives and their families.

Jim's understanding of the purpose of the group was that it served to help kids understand that their parents' breakup was not their fault. He thought it was a "neat" idea, because it's healthy to get things out.

Jim discovered the one thing all the Banana Splits had in common was that they favored one parent over the other. This was usually the father, since the dad was most often the noncustodial parent and, as Jim says, "He brings them on more fun activities and may not be as strict." Tellingly, the kids all agreed that this parental favoritism was a problem, not a virtue. They were honest about their preference, but they understood the importance of having two parents. All but one of the kids loved both parents. And the one thing they all really dreaded was fighting between Mom and Dad.

"We felt a little torn between our parents once in a while," Jim remembers. "Like when they'd fight to see which of them got us during a vacation or something. I know that during my custody trial, I didn't want to say anything bad about my dad because he was my parent and I still loved him, even though I didn't want to live with him."

Jim still harbors pain from his parents' divorce. He's hurt that his father decided to live far away rather than stay near him. He is especially hurt that his father didn't come to his bar mitzvah. But he's never directly confronted his father with his feelings. Jim says he is reluctant to get into any arguments with his father because of what that might mean for Jim's mom.

"I guess I'm scared of my dad," he admits. "Not because he'll say he doesn't want to see me, but because any dispute with me might mean he would stop paying his child support."

Still, Jim doesn't believe divorce is a bad thing as long as the parents reassure their kids that the breakup isn't the children's fault. He knows that people don't get along sometimes, and he doesn't think just having both parents in the same house with you automatically makes you okay.

"I don't know how it is with kids who see both parents more often than I do and are more connected," says Jim, "but I don't want to be with them if they're bickering all the time."

Together, the Banana Splits came up with a hypothesis about their nonnuclear lives that would shock the gloomy divorce doomsayers. These kids believe divorce has actually helped make them better young people, more mature, and more comfortable in social situations. As Jim explains it, "I think you have to grow up faster, you sort of get used to being a child of divorce after a while, and it makes you very good at being social. Like every time I fly to Hawaii to see my Dad, I always walk off the plane with presents from the flight attendants who have become my friends on the way over."

But all the kids were annoyed, often angry, when one parent badmouthed the other one, especially when the criticism was one the kids had no way of proving or disproving. They resented having to wonder whether a parent really did or didn't do what the other parent claimed. Those are "forever questions," Jim says, queries the kids can never really answer.

The children of divorce don't like forever questions much.

The Children of Divorce Bill of Rights, compiled by the Dane County Family Counseling Service of Madison, Wisconsin, includes:

- The right to be treated as important human beings with unique feelings, ideas and desires and not as a source of argument between parents.
- The right to a continuing relationship with both parents and the freedom to receive love from and express love for both.
- The right to express love and affection for each parent without having to stifle that love because of fear of disapproval by the other parent.
- The right to know that their parents' decision to divorce is not their responsibility and that they will live with one parent and visit the other parent.
- The right to continuing care and guidance from both parents.
- The right to honest answers to questions about the changing family relationships.
- The right to know and appreciate what is good in each parent without one parent degrading the other.
- The right to have a relaxed, secure relationship with both parents without being placed in a position to manipulate one parent against the other.
- The right to have the custodial parent not undermine visitation by suggesting tempting alternatives or by threatening to withhold visitation as a punishment for the children's wrongdoing.
- The right to be able to experience regular and consistent visitation and the right to know the reason for a canceled visit.

CHAPTER 3

———— ◆ ————

The Blame Game:
The Emotions of Divorce

The greatest remedy for anger is delay.

—SENECA

Doug Page became a legal legend in the Golden State by successfully representing male clients in California's turbulent divorce courts. When he retired from that pressure cooker in the early 1990s, with the insight of a soldier who survived to see the big picture, he discovered that for twelve years in the trenches he had fought for the wrong reasons. Like any good lawyer, Page's goal was to win: to save his clients money, to win them custody, or just to make sure they had more than their ex-wives after the law dust settled. But he is now convinced that in order to be a good father, divorced dads have to act very unmanly. They have to submit.

They must put making money second. They must refrain from attack and do whatever they can to cooperate with their children's mothers. Most important, they have to redefine what it means to be a man, resisting pressure from both extremes, the one that expects them to swagger through life like John Wayne and the opposite end of the spectrum that expects them to tiptoe through life like a bad imitation of a woman.

And nowhere is this inner struggle fought more fiercely than in the area of emotions.

Unhooked from a Feeling

Will was twenty-one years old when he married. His wife was a few years younger. They had their whole life ahead of them—and Will's wife knew exactly how it would go. She immediately put her plans for the future into action by becoming pregnant. Eventually they would have six kids.

Everything in his marriage was decided by Will's wife: their religious preference, the church they attended, the job he took, where they lived. Will liked the arrangement for a while, because he felt secure wrapped in his wife's unblinking certainty about how their lives should go. But after six or seven years, he began to get mysteriously depressed. At first he didn't know why.

One day Will realized something: he was just along for the ride in his marriage. Certainty wasn't enough anymore. After several heroic attempts at salvaging their union, he and his wife divorced.

To this day, she doesn't really understand what happened, and you can't blame her. Will never really made it clear what was going on his head. He calls himself a "hold-in-my-feelings typical guy," and this male instinct has caused him and his kids no end of grief.

His children were blindsided by the breakup. One of them used to watch divorced couples in the movies or on television and plaintively ask his parents, "You aren't going to separate are you?" They would laugh and say, "Of course not." They never even hinted to the kids that there was anything wrong with the marriage. So the kids were stunned and devastated when their mother took them aside one day while they were waiting for dad to return from a business trip, and announced that she and their father were getting divorced.

These poor kids were crushed. But they all hid their feelings—just like their dad—and the effort has cost them. One of Will's youngest children, for example, manifested his pain medically, suffering recurring rounds of migraine headaches. Others are still in denial about how they were affected by their parents' divorce, and it's been five years since the breakup.

I believe Will's behavior was standard for an American man. Expressing emotion is not considered masculine in this country except under very specific circumstances, and especially not where divorce is concerned. It's okay, even expected, for a divorced man to express anger at the end of his marriage, and in these politically correct times he is even allowed a small to moderate amount of sadness, but any other kind of emoting is strictly forbidden.

The stereotypical guy thing to do when you get divorced is to take it like a man and move on. Have a beer with your buddies and tell horror stories about life with "the witch." Complain about how alimony is bleeding you dry. Admit that the separation will be tough on the kids but "they'll adjust." Buy a sports car and start dating an aerobics instructor named Kimberly. The problem is, none of these techniques help, and some, with their potential for public humiliation, can make the situation worse.

A man feels many things after the breakup of his marriage besides anger and sadness. Even his instincts on how to handle those two emotions are probably ineffective at best and liable to blow up in his face at worst. Continuing to vent rage by fighting with a former wife is almost guaranteed to make a guy feel worse than he already does, and almost certainly will screw up his kids. Remaining in the divorce equivalent of a shooting war long after the marriage is over is akin to deliberately choosing to remain miserable for years.

As for the sadness a divorced dad is most likely feeling, he may be reluctant or even adamantly opposed to expressing it, especially to his male friends. But holding in that intensely negative feeling now is like putting a down payment on a psychological explosion later. Facing all of this, unfortunately, is easier said than done, especially if a divorced father is struggling with the most uncomfortable emotion of all—humiliation.

"I am writing here because I am too humiliated to tell my local friends what has happened," one poor devil posted on the Internet. "I thought that my marriage was doing OK. A couple of nights ago, my spouse tells me she is leaving. I beg her to consider counseling but she rejects that. We had never even argued! I am beside myself."

Our favorite source of misinformation, the American media, delights in giving us caricatures of the pathetic middle-aged man who dumps his loyal but aging wife for a young chippie. In truth, most marriages are ended by the wife—some estimates go as high as 75 percent. Of course, many of these women leave their spouses precisely because the man committed adultery, or was verbally or physically abusive. It's hard to find sympathy for these men. They probably deserve to feel like heels.

Nevertheless, whatever caused the dissolution of your marriage, hanging on to feeling rotten about your divorce is guaranteed to mess up your future relationships. You may feel compelled to jump from one affair to another. Even more damaging, you may become emotionally needy, clinging to your kids for solace. Custodial and noncustodial parents alike frequently seek to restore their damaged self-esteem by focusing too much on their children, becoming emotionally dependent on them. Fathers are less overt about this than mothers, but they do it too, and it isn't healthy for anybody.

Another demon unleashed by divorce is guilt, the emotion

with which men are arguably least prepared to cope (unless, of course, they're Catholic or Jewish, but that's another book). Expressing guilt, after all, is admitting empathy, which is a difficult thing for us "manly" types to do.

Your divorce emotions can be savage in their intensity, ripping you up inside like a Florida palm tree whipped by hurricane-force winds. Chances are, the failure of your marriage will affect you more than anything else that ever happens to you in your life.

Believe it or not, that's normal.

According to the Social Readjustment Rating Scale, developed in the late 1960s by social scientists T. H. Holmes and R. H. Rahe to measure the degree of dislocation created by various life events, divorce is second only to the death of a spouse in its power to change your life—well ahead of such stresses as being fired from work or changes in financial condition.

Do Not Bring to a Boil: Handling Anger

Sometime in the past couple of decades, anger hired a really good press agent. Nowadays we're told that anger is a natural emotion, perfectly logical under the right circumstances, and therefore an acceptable male expression of emotion. We are further advised that anger contained corrupts its container—you have to get it out or it will eat you up. Go to the gym. Take a run. Better yet, yell at your ex-wife. You'll feel so much better.

It's not that simple.

The key truth you haven't been told, but must accept, is that getting angry doesn't work. When you get angry, you lose. Expressing anger at an ex-spouse is like pouring gasoline on a fire. You could run a marathon, and you'll still be pissed off when you're finished, only a lot more tired. And the fire will still be burning.

Certainly divorced dads can find great justification for anger during and after divorce. Divorce often brings out the worst in people, turning former lovers into malicious insult machines. In addition, if they're fathers in any sense of the word at all, men find themselves sacrificing their own desires and economic stability for the good of their children—in other words, they're sacrificing everything they've worked for.

Then there are the real zingers that strike at the very heart of your self-identity. When a guy's been cuckolded, for example, who can blame him for his fury? And the financial burden alimony and child support place on many divorced men (almost never mentioned because of its political incorrectness) would make even the most saintly ex-husband growl. Just under fifty-four cents of every dollar I made went to my ex-wife in the year or two following our divorce—and she's an executive in a securities company, not a stay-at-home mom. That, my lawyer told me, was the "conventional" percentage of alimony and child support paid by men in California. My dad had to help me out at first, a galling experience for a man in his late thirties. In my daybook, I reminded myself when it was time to pay the ex with the notation "blood money."

Even if a divorced dad is not economically squeezed, he's still likely to feel a great deal of restless, unfocused rage when a marriage ends, due to the scope of the consequences and how hugely divorce looms on the landscape of an individual's life.

It's true that anger is a psychological defense mechanism. We get angry when we've been wronged—that's an appropriate response. But we can express even appropriate anger in unhealthy ways. Anyway, too much of the anger divorced people express is neither healthy nor well-targeted. It springs from somewhere else, and it usually inflames the situation rather than resolving it.

My ex, Livia, phoned one day in late October to tell me she was taking Alex to New York in a month to visit relatives for Thanksgiving. She said she might also make a side trip to Orlando to take Alex to Disney World. I asked her in an accusing voice why she was going. Now, button-pushed, Livia pushed back, announcing, "I don't need your permission to do anything," and adding, "I may be thinking about moving to Florida." Then she hung up.

Anger begot anger. The purpose of her call was courtesy, to inform me of her plans well in advance so we could rearrange visitation times. Her tone, at least initially, hadn't been accusatory or insulting, and her plans weren't unusual, except that she was going out of town. Traditionally, Alex spends Thanksgiving with his mom's parents because they live near us in southern California and my family lives back East. And of course, she really wasn't planning to move out of state.

So why did I get angry? I'm not sure. Some old wound from the marriage resurfacing, probably. Thanksgiving week is when we first split up, and at that time Livia and Alex did fly back East for the holiday, so maybe the conversation hit a little too close to the bone for me. The point is, I think everybody is just a little on edge when talking to the ex; it doesn't take much, or even anything, to set us off. The point is, my anger was inappropriate and misdirected. It didn't make me feel better. In fact, it created an unnecessary argument and put me in the position of having to apologize to my ex, and most divorced dads would rather swallow paint thinner than do that.

Even when your anger is justified and she deserves it, what does rage ever accomplish except to make your face unattractively red or give you a momentary tingle of vindication? Getting angry is not some unavoidable instinct, like jumping off a cliff if you're a lemming. Anger is a method, just one out of several for handling situations that hurt you. You'll get better results—especially where your kids' well-being is concerned—if you bargain with your ex instead. You don't have to like your opponent to make peace with her.

Indeed, the ability to rechannel anger into more constructive avenues may be the most necessary skill a divorced dad needs to make postdivorce parenting work. We'll discuss how to handle anger with your ex in more detail in the next chapter.

Blame Me: Getting Out of the Guilt Trap

Michael Oddenino is a tireless advocate for children's rights, a respected authority on parenting, an author, a lecturer, and an accomplished counsel for divorced dads. But even Michael had to pause when I asked him how his male clients handle their guilt over the breakup of their marriages.

"I don't see that much," Oddenino admitted. "Mostly I see anger."

That response surfaced almost every time I interviewed a lawyer for this book. It's one of the most revealing patterns I uncovered in the divorced dad's reality. Attorneys see only anger from divorced males. Or perhaps they just don't recognize other factors at work. Researchers and psychologists also tend to focus on the anger generated on both sides by the death of a marriage. But any good man suffers some remorse from his divorce, and many suffer greatly.

Sometimes the guilt has an obvious cause: the man cheated on his wife. Sometimes it's more subtle: he believes he let the family down by allowing the marriage to disintegrate.

Men who initiated their divorce or whose marriage broke up because they cheated on their wives will often act out their guilt by becoming overly magnanimous. They take on the role of martyr and make grand, self-righteous gestures to set things right. This is one way men try to hold on to their image of themselves as defenders of the hearth. They'll give their wives everything they have because material things don't matter anymore. They've discovered what's really important in life.

The problem is, they haven't. They're just acting out—accepting blame for something that really is nobody's fault. Marriages break up for a panoply of reasons and rarely because of one person's behavior. (Obviously, this doesn't apply to tragedies in which one of the parents is psychologically unstable, an alcoholic, or an addict.)

Well-known psychologists, radio co-hosts, and husband and wife Ann Christie and Leslie Pam often tell listeners struggling with the effects of divorce that the best way to extinguish behavior is to ignore it. You expect to feel lots of guilt, but you don't act it out. Pam offers another suggestion for divorced dads, one I believe is crucial for good men to follow but difficult to accept: forgive yourself. I know that sounds like new age silliness, but it really is essential, and more important, it works.

Everybody makes mistakes. What matters is how you handle your mistakes, not that you failed to be perfect. If you resist the temptation to do things just to make amends to your no-longer nuclear family and instead strive to be a strong and loving father to your kids and a dependable co-parenting partner with your ex-wife, you can actually turn the negative of divorced male guilt into a positive role model message for your children. What they're going to take away from observing you is not that you did something wrong, but how you dealt with adversity.

If you're going to be any good at all to your children, it's imperative that you *recognize and get over the guilt you feel over the breakup of your marriage*. You may not always be aware that you have guilt, however. Remember, it is not a guy thing, and you can easily fool yourself. But if you find yourself shelling out a lot of money for things the kids and the ex can do very well without, if you find yourself constantly defending your ex to your friends and confidantes with expressions like "I'm no angel" or "You have to understand her," you're probably overcompensating for guilt.

The divorce wasn't her fault. It wasn't yours either. She had her reasons. So did you.

Move on.

The Failure Factor

Adam was a successful young government official with a pretty wife and a baby daughter. Active in his Pacific Northwest community, Adam was living the American dream. Then the roof caved in. Adam and his wife decided to separate.

Adam's stay was sadly familiar: he didn't share his feelings with his wife, and so he never confronted her about what he saw as her insensitivity to his desires and dreams for their life together. So when she suddenly wanted out, he was stunned. Although he gamely went through the conventional male motions of preparing for a life change, moving to a small apartment and sending out resumés for jobs in other cities, Adam couldn't accept what was happening to him. His entire existence revolved around his wife and child. They were his only family and he was losing them.

One night about three weeks into the separation, it all came crashing down on him. As rain fell softly outside his window, Adam sat at his desk, staring with teary eyes at a loaded .38 revolver. As he reached for the pistol, the phone rang. The call was routine, about setting up a job interview. But it saved the young man's life. Adam, believing the timely call was an omen, put the gun away and resolved to go through with the divorce and rebuild his life. Now happily remarried, Adam still shakes when he recalls the power his divorce-induced despair had over him.

Adam's experience is a dramatic illustration that most men really aren't strong, silent types and shouldn't be expected to play that role. Unfortunately, most guys don't really believe that, so it's not uncommon for divorcing men to have suicidal impulses. We are, after all, the parent who usually leaves, we're the one giving up our friends, our house, daily contact with our children, our psychological support systems. Males are most often the parents who end up alone after a divorce.

This explains at least in part why studies show divorced men remarry more quickly than divorced women.

Many men feel that their job as husband and father is to win bread for their brood, protect the wife and kids from a harsh and dangerous world, and run their mortgaged castle with a firm but fair patriarchal hand. Divorce, no matter what the individual circumstances of a situation may be, implies that the man wasn't good enough to do any of that. Intellectually, he may understand that the measure of a man can't be taken by whether his marriage stays intact. Divorce isn't a contest. Keeping score, however, is how most males determine their place in the world. Emotionally, therefore, they feel that they've lost the game of life when their marriage is over. The marriage, in fact, may be the foundation upon which their entire identity rests, as it was with Adam.

The sadness, the sense of failure as a man, can be so overwhelming that some divorced fathers respond by removing themselves from their children's lives completely.

If you have even the slightest urge to do this, don't. If you've already done it, undo it. I don't care how far away you live or what the circumstances of your divorce may be. You are not only doing incalculable damage to your children, you are hurting yourself more profoundly than your ex-wife or your kids could ever hurt you.

One day almost twenty years ago, John came home from a weekend business trip and found an empty home. It was a shock because although he knew his wife was unhappy with some aspects of their marriage, divorce had never really been discussed. Such a conversation probably wouldn't have lasted very long anyway, because John, like many men, is uncomfortable talking about such things. So he was thunderstruck when he found himself alone in a deserted house.

He walked from room to room, stunned by the silence. He knew where his wife had gone; she'd taken their two girls to her mother's house. Still, it was days before he contacted them.

John felt betrayed in the most brutal way. He saw only one

way to ease the pain. He left town, his job, and his two daughters. He communicated with them a few times a year and saw them even less, and their lives veered further and further apart.

That was many years ago, but John still regrets his decision.

"The most important thing is to continue to raise your children even in circumstances which are wildly different from what you expected when you entered into the relationship [with your ex-wife]," he says. "I continue to have difficulty putting my first marriage and its demise into a box. But I think concern for the children has got to be paramount. That has to subsume whatever feelings of bitterness attend the divorce. I think you have to keep trying, and it's real hard. It's awfully easy to find excuses, if not to give up, then to take, to accept, a diminished role in the children's welfare.

"Related to that, maybe I didn't do at all well. I sincerely regret having taken the easy way out. It's hard to imagine feeling lower than I felt in the immediate aftermath of my divorce, but as bad as things get, they do get better. It is possible to pick up the pieces and put them back together. And with some luck, you put them back together in some pretty interesting and unique ways."

John has put his life back together. He's remarried and is the father of a bright and lively towheaded little boy. John also has made an effort to rebuild his relationship with his daughters, who are now young adults, and although more emotional distance than he would like remains between them, they have welcomed him back in their lives.

Why wouldn't they? He's their dad.

Take the Offered Hand

I'm not overly fond of researchers and I am skeptical, to say the least, of their tendency to study a length of trunk or a foot of tusk and then make sweeping pronouncements about the nature of elephants. Nevertheless, I have to admit that research can save lives. I know it because that's what finally saved Adam, our lonely divorced dad in the Pacific Northwest.

Two professors at the university where Adam worked had applied to the government for federal funding to study divorced fathers. A reply came back quickly, with a quarter of a million dollars. (This was the 1970s, when there was no research of any kind on fathers, let alone divorced fathers.) The two academics then set up study groups of divorced fathers designed as encounter sessions in which the men helped one another deal with their "aloneness." Adam was one of those men, and he maintains that the ability to talk about his feelings with other divorced men saved his life.

Every divorced dad who has sought help—anywhere and from anyone—swears by its benefits. Those who didn't seek out someone to talk to about the end of their marriage say they should have. When asked to add one final word of advice to readers of this book, John, our distanced father of two daughters, chose to admonish divorced dads to find someone they can talk to about what they're going through and what they're feeling.

That means really talking about what's going on with you, not just sitting down with someone over a beer in a bar and puffing yourself up with bluster. Your kids need help to cope with divorce and you can't go it alone either, so don't try. It's impossible to see the forest for the trees when the whole damn forest has just gone up in flames.

Greg, whose wife left him for another man, realized he needed someone to talk to. Though he doesn't consider himself an open person emotionally, he found that it helped to talk with someone neutral, who wasn't going to challenge him and from whom there would be no repercussions. He also intentionally sought out a female therapist so that he could get a feel for "the other side of the coin."

This is not some warm and fuzzy, 1990s-guy kind of counsel. This is vital for you as a man to restore your self-respect. The advice Leslie Pam gives the many divorced fathers who call his radio show is characteristically blunt, but every divorced dad ought to take it to heart.

"The thing we constantly hear from guys," Pam says, "is 'She worked me over; I feel like a piece of dog meat; she's taken the kids and all the money; I can't talk to her; she's out screwing around with other guys and I have no control over this thing; my kids are getting worked over completely and totally and I just don't know what to do.'

"We tell them to get into a men's support group and get their balls back. I tell them that on the air. Don't lose your balls."

Harsh, but accurate. Your choice of an ally or allies doesn't have to be a licensed therapist or an encounter group. You'll be just as well served (and maybe better) by confiding in a best friend who won't judge you. That's who I leaned on in the dismal months just after my marriage ended. Your confidante also can be a member of your family. She can be a female friend whose opinion you value. In fact, you can turn to anyone you respect and are willing to listen to.

Sure, your married friends might not be the soul of sensitivity—my two best friends' advice to me postdivorce can be summed up in three words: "Go get laid." Family members might be too intent on vindicating their low opinion of your ex-wife to really pay attention to how much you hurt. But you can find a shoulder to lean on somewhere. You'd be surprised how useful it can be.

One divorced dad had the good fortune to have a mom with a Ph.D. in education to lean on. His mother maintained a friendly relationship with his ex-wife, so she was able to act as a go-between in the predictably rocky first two years after the divorce. She spent time with his kids during the week, helping provide continuity in their lives. When one of this good man's children couldn't adjust to the transition to a one-parent home and started having crying fits in school, Grandma volunteered to help out in the little girl's classroom one day a week, which helped reduce the child's separation anxiety. And she did that for an entire semester.

Not every divorced dad is blessed with Wonder Woman for a mother, but we all have someone we can turn to if we just think about it. More formal help is available through parent education classes. We don't usually think of this kind of training for divorced parents, but they need it just as much as couples expecting their first child. Indeed, divorced parents may need formalized guidance even more than nondivorced parents, since there are so many more potential pitfalls in raising children in a sundered home.

When his daughter was eight years old, divorced dad Mark Ludwick, who shared physical custody of little Stephanie with his wife, took a parent education course offered by his church. He was a little reluctant at first, but he soon found to his delight that the course was invaluable. He took more courses, then more, about $400 worth in all, and eventually he began teaching effective parenting to others.

In 1993 honor roll college student Stephanie Ludwick got an excited phone call from her dad. She needed to fly down to North Carolina with him—Mark had just been named International Single Parent of the Year by the single-parent group Parents Without Partners. In accepting his award, Ludwick credited the honor to his daughter, but he later confided that "if it weren't for the classes and me applying what I learned, Steph wouldn't have been as good a kid as she turned out to be and I wouldn't have won the award."

Ten years ago, it was rare for municipalities to offer parenting classes, but today the Association for Family and Conciliation Courts estimates that more than forty states offer court-affiliated parent education programs for divorcing parents. Some states, including Utah and Connecticut, even require such classes before they'll grant a divorce.

A study in Utah found that seven out of ten divorcing parents resented having to take mandatory parent education. After completing the classes, however, 95 percent said they were really glad they had participated. So there are other options besides wallowing in your misery. Getting help may seem too bitter a pill to swallow, but it's guaranteed to make you and your kids feel better.

Don't Dwell on Divorce

The final piece of advice divorced dads need to hear is one you might not think is appropriate for men: *don't obsess about your divorce.* Divorced dads may be adept at hiding their own feelings from themselves, but even so, they can dwell too much on what has happened to them and neglect job one: getting on with their lives and with being a good father to their kids. John, for example, has always been haunted by that empty house he came home to, and his obsession with the way his marriage ended led to his decision to distance himself from his girls.

There are any number of reasons that a marriage breaks up. Don't try to put your divorce in a neat little box. Life is messy and you just spilled all over the carpet. If you keep trying to find that one big reason, you'll never get over your divorce. So learn from your mistake, figure out how not to do it again, teach that to your kids, clean up the mess, and move on.

CHAPTER 4

———————— ◆ ————————

The Right Connections:
How to Be an Involved Dad

> To give of one's self; to leave the world a bit better,
> whether by a healthy child, a garden patch or a re-
> deemed social condition; to have played and
> laughed with enthusiasm and sung with exultation;
> to know even one life has breathed easier because
> you have lived—this is to have succeeded.
>
> —RALPH WALDO EMERSON

When he was in the fifth grade, Martin's parents decided on
the first of three separations that would eventually lead to
divorce. Martin, who had been a pianist of great promise,
reacted to the split by refusing to have anything more to do
with music. He wouldn't even touch the piano. Although
previously a well-behaved student, he soon became a constant disruption in class. The final straw was when he

brought a mirror to class and kept shining it in his teacher's face, blinding him.

Although they were in the midst of a wrenching and emotional parting, Martin's parents submerged their feelings toward each other and worked out a plan of action with the principal of Martin's school. Realizing that their separation was the problem, both parents made it plain to their young son that what was happening was not his fault and would not cost him either parent. Martin improved to such a degree that at the end of the year, the principal sent both parents notes thanking them for their diligent efforts on behalf of their son.

But despite coming together for their son's sake, this couple just couldn't make their marriage work. By the end of their third separation, Martin was mediating their disputes, and even he was telling his parents they should get divorced. As a consequence, Martin feels he missed out on part of his childhood—he can't remember much of it, in fact, which he attributes to the pressure of having to come between his warring parents. And he admits that the divorce made him act "wild and screwed up."

Eventually Martin and his mother moved to the West Coast and his father moved to the Midwest. Ten years after Martin's parents decided to split up for the first time, a standing room only crowd that included several music company executives packed the legendary Whisky nightclub on Sunset Boulevard to hear a hot new band showcase its act. It was a triumphant night for the young musicians, especially their lead singer—Martin.

But this story doesn't have quite as happy an ending as we'd like. Martin's dad didn't make the showcase. It was one of many times in Martin's life when his dad didn't make it for some significant event.

Martin's dad used to take him fishing, although his father really didn't like to fish all that much. But he knew it was important to his son. After a while, though, Martin's father stopped doing that. Martin noticed. He noticed other things, too. Like when Martin was at a boarding school in Minne-apolis, his father lived close by. But when they arranged a visit, he wouldn't pick up Martin himself. He'd send a limo. When Martin got to his dad's place, his father would work the whole time. And when the boy had his wisdom teeth pulled, his father arranged for Martin's grandparents to pick him up and take him home.

Martin's dad wasn't only physically absent, he was also absent emotionally. And that absence created a deep hurt in the boy. You can hear it in his voice and see it in his eyes when he talks about his father.

"When a kid grows up, he's gonna relate to his father," Martin says now. "His mother may understand him better but the boy is going to look to his father for guidance and leadership, as the guy who takes him out to throw the foot-ball around. It's important that the father share things from his past, to show his son that he understands."

It wasn't so much the divorce of his parents that hurt Mar-tin, but rather his father's decision, conscious or unconscious, to not participate fully in his son's life.

In all the interviews I conducted for this book, the most poignant comments came from sons whose divorced dads were physically and emotionally distant. Every one of these kids, who ranged in age from eight or nine to twenty years old, reacted the same way. They'd say the divorce hadn't affected them much, but then, speaking in unemotional voices, they'd relate all the little things their dads didn't do with them, all the small life moments their fathers weren't there for, just like Martin's father, and you could feel the pain hidden behind those flat tones.

The need for a father to remain fully engaged in his kids' lives is particularly acute in the first months or even years after a divorce; it becomes almost a test of his love in his children's eyes. No matter how often he's with his kids, a divorced dad is going to have to do some serious reassuring. For one thing, he's usually the one who physically leaves the household. For another, his departure deprives his kids of what psychologist and divorce expert Dr. Neil Kalter calls "atmosphere of father-presence," that omnipresent, invisible security blanket a child happily wraps around himself or herself when Dad lives at home. Even if he's not physically with them all the time, the nearby presence of their father imbues children with an almost primal sense of safety.

So the kids watch and evaluate. Daddy says he loves us and isn't leaving forever, but we'll see. Is he really going to be our daddy anymore? Some children even count the hours or days of visitation, keeping score on how deeply their dad is committed to them. Even five years after my divorce, my son still does that.

"You Can't Make Me Go"

The security knife, however, can cut both ways. If you're a divorced dad with very young children, there's a better than even chance that at the beginning of your divorce, your youngster got hysterical when it was time to go back to Mom. But your little one may also have gotten hysterical about leaving Mom's house when you showed up for visitation weekend. It's difficult not to gloat when you're the beneficiary of this behavior or spiral into the depths of depression when you're its target, but both reactions are unnecessary. This is one of the ways the children of divorce react to change. It's not an indictment of either parent, and the behavior eventually passes.

Divorced dads don't have to passively endure it, however. For the first year after my divorce, my son would explode into tears every time I brought him back to his mom at the end of my weekends. It broke my heart and drove a dagger through his mother's as well, but we just kept calmly explaining to him that I'd still be around and he'd see me soon.

One time, however, the tables turned. Alex was playing with my ex and her boyfriend when I came to pick him up. He was having fun, basking in the simulated "nuclear family glow." Being only three years old, he naturally resented being wrenched away from the good times. When we tried to get him to leave with me, he sat on the floor and began to howl. The look on my face melted even my ex-wife; she tried for another ten minutes to get Alex to calm down, to no avail.

Crushed, I left alone. I drove maybe a quarter of a mile and parked the car to think. No, this was wrong, I thought. I couldn't set this precedent. He was my son too.

I turned the car around and returned to their house. "Look," I told Alex, "when you're a teenager you can decide what to do with your weekends. But not now. I'm your dad, and you stay with me every other weekend. You can play with Gary when you come back."

Out we went, Alex still sniffling. My ex-wife and the boyfriend smiled at me as I shut the door; they were as relieved as I was. Five minutes into the ride back to my house, Alex had forgotten all about the tantrum and was his usual happy self. We never had a problem with visitation—coming or going—again.

I believe that incident demonstrated to my little boy, in a way that he could understand, that not only was I there for him, but I was prepared to fight to remain his father. (It is also vitally important to stress that my ex-wife was firmly and explicitly on my side through the whole thing.)

You've got to show your kids that you are committed to them. And some dads will go to extraordinary lengths to demonstrate that commitment.

Will, the divorced father of six, went to extraordinary lengths to prove his devotion to his kids. When his ex-wife decided to remarry, Will rearranged his job so he wouldn't have to travel so much, then attempted to get custody of his children—all six of them. He knew he wouldn't win, but that wasn't the point. He was afraid that his ex-wife would move away after her second marriage (she did), and he needed to show his kids that their dad cared about them. Will understood that a fight would do nobody any good. Nevertheless, he felt he had to send a message of caring and love and interest. They had to know that he hadn't divorced them.

And you know, he was probably right. His relationship with his kids remained strong even though they did subsequently move hundreds of miles away. He was, in effect, teaching his brood about loyalty and commitment, and when a dad leads by example that way, you can almost see his kids glow.

Getting Your Attention

Perhaps the most ironic aspect of fathering is that dads frequently get better at it after they're divorced. All those fishing trips you put off, all those times you decided you'd go to the zoo next month, all the time you had to do all those things is gone. Suddenly you're divorced and there's no time left.

This is a rough lesson but one well-learned. After the marriage breaks up, you savor every chance you have to be with your children, especially if you live far away and don't see your kids often. And you don't just value time with your kids more, you become far more aware of the value of the time. In other words, you start paying attention.

"You take your kids for granted just like you do your marriage sometimes," says Gary, separated almost three years, with two young sons aged six and eight. "When my wife and I were together, I was working a lot of hours and either I was too tired to play with the boys when I got home or I got home too late and they were already asleep. Now that I'm divorced, I schedule times to be with my kids just like I schedule business meetings. And I really look forward to those times. I also find the time to be involved in Cub Scouts and soccer and all the things they were doing that I didn't think I had time for when I was married."

Enthusiastically participating in your kids' activities is probably one of the best ways you can be an involved dad.

Alex Feuer, aka "The Terminator," scourge of the West Valley Junior Soccer League (Division 6), stands in the middle of the muddy field like a four-foot tall fire hydrant in shorts. Rushing down on him are several opposing players. As they approach, The Terminator does what he always does in the heat of battle.

He ducks.

The attackers sweep by him and smash the ball into the net for the winning score. On the sidelines, Alex's mom is screaming at him. His grandparents are screaming at him. All the other parents of the kids on our team are screaming at him. Alex, misinterpreting the noise, raises his chubby little fist in triumph.

In the coach's box across the field, I remain silent. In my head, however, I've just crossed off "pro soccer player" from my list of Things I Want My Son to Be.

The Terminator, of course, has already forgotten his brush with athletic destiny and is racing as fast as his stocky little legs can carry him to the sidelines for the traditional post-game fruit juice and cookies.

When my ex suggested I volunteer to be assistant coach of my son's soccer team, my imagination ran amok. Trophies lining the shelf in Alex's room . . . Breathless articles in the local paper describing his latest exploits . . . and the bonding! Lord, the bonding we'd do.

Bonding, as we all know, is even more critical when you're a divorced dad. You gotta grab the moments when you can. And Alex's mom, bless her strange little heart, understands this. In fact, that's why she suggested the coaching gig.

But Alex on a soccer field is a still-life. A tree growing. Unless, of course, the ball is anywhere near him. Which is when he ducks. Of course, those precious life moments that sports are supposed to provide fathers and sons never go as planned.

Alex failed to make the all-star team. He was the only one surprised by this. After the last game, I took him and his mother to Red Robin in the hopes that chicken fingers and French fries would console him somewhat. He ate the fingers and fries, but remained down on himself. So I went to the

Dad Manual and pulled out some surefire homilies: "Not making the all-star team doesn't mean you're a bad player, son. Besides, if you try real hard, you'll make the team next year."

Hearing this, The Terminator snorted. Bits of French fry flew across the table. With increasing desperation, I went back to the Dad Manual. It said, "Try a my-life-as-metaphor story." I'd never tried a my-life-as-metaphor story before.

"Alex," I began, "when I was eleven, I wasn't picked for the all-star softball team at camp. I was disappointed, just like you."

Another snort, louder and more emphatic than the first. Chicken fingers scattered across the restaurant floor like raindrops in a hurricane.

"That's your life," he said in disgust. "It's not my life. I've gotta live my life."

Now there were *two* disconsolate males at the table. And the only thing my ex could do was smile at me in sympathy. Athletics is Dad's turf. Doesn't matter if Dad lives at home or not. He's the go-to guy in the sports bonding department. And I had just dropped the ball.

But the next week when I picked Alex up for the weekend, he jumped into my arms and asked, "Daddy, are you going to be our coach again next year?"

"Sure am, pal."

"Outstanding," said The Terminator. "I can't wait for the season to start!"

Sometimes it doesn't matter whether you win or lose, or even how you play the game. Sometimes all you have to do is be there.

Last year 10 million kids participated in soccer and baseball leagues around the country, many of them coached by their own dads. I don't know how many of those fathers were divorced, but however many there were, their kids will forever be grateful to them.

Fathers help prepare their children, daughters and sons, for the future. Team sports can help dads teach their kids verities about honor, loyalty, hard work, and fair play. Serving as a coach also shows kids that Dad is a leader, an authority figure, which is particularly important to children of divorce.

So coach your kid's soccer, or Little League, or Pop Warner team. Not only will you be giving your own kids a great gift they will keep as a treasured memory their whole lives, you will be helping yourself as well. The sense of satisfaction you feel teaching young boys and girls how to play a game, how to be proud in defeat and generous in victory, is extraordinary. Faced with thirteen or fourteen expectant young faces on a practice field, you'll also learn much about fathering.

Plus you get those really neat T-shirts that say "Coach" on the breast pocket.

But coaching isn't the only way you can use sports to be involved with your kids. Just showing up at all their games and working with them to improve their pitching, passing, and shooting, can also bring you together. And it's always fun to attend professional sporting events together.

Growing up, I had a rather ambivalent relationship with my own father. He was very "old world" and somewhat authoritarian. He was also extremely successful in everything he did. I loved him, but I also resented him. And over the years I learned that about the only area in which we could relate to each other was sports. I vividly remember a time when I was three years old. My father took me to a baseball game and I got to shake hands with Willie Mays. For me, that's a special Dad Memory I will never forget. It's one of the few times I felt that I really bonded with him.

See and Be Seen

Whenever Tom's two sons are out of school or absent, he's the parent the school secretaries call. "Oh, I'm sorry to bother you," they'll say, "but you're the only one who seems to know what's going on."

That in-depth involvement in his boys' lives is what won Tom joint physical custody when he took his ex-wife to court. A happy ending? Sure, but the point is, Tom had to prove he was committed to being an involved father. The perception still exists out there in the real world that fathers aren't actively interested in their children. The Tender Years still lurks in the halls of your child's school, in his pediatrician's waiting room, and on the playground at daycare.

Make no mistake about it: if you are a divorced father, whatever your legal arrangement is, it is critical that the authority figures in your child's life know who you are. Once he is divorced, a man's access to his children and his ability to parent depend heavily on outside opinions. That includes his children's teachers, doctors, school principals, maybe even the head of the PTA. If they don't know you, they will assume you don't care about your kids, so do not follow your instinct and leave these things up to your ex-wife. *You must be personally and continually involved in your children's lives outside the home.*

As Tom says, "The world has to see you seeing your kids all the time."

You can find assistance from an unlikely source: the family courts. The policy of most states is that unless there's a court order to the contrary, *a father has the right to access his child's school, medical, and dental records.* You should demand a parent/teacher conference, on your own or with your ex-wife. Visit your kid's school. Get to know the principal. Make sure you have access to report cards. Get on the mailing list for the school activities calendar.

There may be red tape involved. You might have to write a letter to the school specifying what records you want to see, or the school might require some other procedure for noncustodial parents. Do it. In addition, call the school office at the beginning of the school year and make sure they know you and have your phone number. Make sure you have all the proper permission to be informed about field trips, special events, and after-school activities. I'd even recommend joining the PTA if you have time, especially if your ex-wife is uncooperative about keeping you in the educational loop.

Unless your child is covered under your medical policy, the bureaucratic maze can be time-consuming and annoying when you request to see your kids' medical records or try to get them in to see a doctor or dentist. Health maintenance organizations, for example, are notorious about giving non-custodial parents a hard time, even when an injured child is involved. Call the HMO, find out its procedures, and follow them. You don't want to find yourself in the emergency room one night arguing on the phone with a supervisor or being placed on eternal hold while your kid is in agony because he put his finger on a hot stove after you told him not to.

Finally, *make a point of being there for your kid during non-visitation times.* Let's put one hoary old cliché about good parenting to use here: show up at your child's school play. Spend two minutes after it's over to congratulate your little guy. Attend your daughter's baseball game, even if it isn't your weekend. Take five minutes to tell her she pitched a great game. And don't just call to say "happy birthday." Go to the party, if only for a few minutes. (See Chapter Seven for more about birthday parties.)

Unfortunately, some ex-wives will object to these extra-visitation meetings. But if you behave yourself, and don't start a fight or cause a disruption, you are perfectly within your rights. Barring a restraining order, you are not violating visitation or custody decrees by doing what any good parent would do. If you're worried that you might have difficulty with your child's mother about this, bring someone with you to these events. They can serve as witnesses that you didn't do anything wrong. The custodial parent cannot stop you from doing the right thing in this case. If she does, you don't have to let her get away with it.

There's a second reason for getting involved with your child's life in this way, and while it has nothing to do with custody strategy, it may be even more essential to your post-divorce role. You do all the things we've just described because you want your kids' approval as much as they want yours. If you don't take them to get their shots or show up when they're playing the Tin man in *The Wizard of Oz*, your kids won't recognize you as a caring parent. And in a sense you won't be, no matter what else you do.

Damned if You Do: The Career Choice

Gary has learned that to be a good parent, a divorced dad has to develop the point of view that his kids come first. Really first. Not as in "I have to work extra hard so I can buy you a bicycle and video games." But first as in, "I'm there for important events in their lives and I have time to do the everyday activities with them too." You can't be involved halfway in a youngster's life.

Single custodial moms make a lot of tangible sacrifices for their kids: free time, career opportunities, a spontaneous social life. Dads, however, pay a heavy psychological price to stay close to their children Our culture still doesn't fully accept men who set aside or even abandon their own ambitions to help their children realize their dreams.

During women's history month in 1995, feminist Karen DeCrow was asked to give a speech before a crowd of one hundred top executives of a major multinational corporation. She asked this high-powered bunch if their company had a parental leave program.

They certainly did, she was told. And, DeCrow wanted to know, did women who had children take parental leave? Well, they hadn't done any studies, the executives said, but yes, they believed that was the case. Having set them up with these jabs, DeCrow then delivered the haymaker:

"Do most men in this company who become parents also take parental leave?" she asked.

Laughter.

"Has anyone in this room taken parental leave?"

No one had. They seemed to vaguely recall that there

might have been one man in their company who did take
parental leave once, but nobody knew him personally and
they couldn't remember his name or in what branch of the
company he worked.

DeCrow then asked her audience why men don't take
leave when they become parents.

"Well, they don't want to," was the immediate response.

Later that week when DeCrow spoke at the Children's
Rights Council's National Conference in Washington, D.C.,
she said, "You don't have to be bright to figure out that
everyone in that corporation thought if a man took parental
leave, he wasn't a heavy hitter. He wasn't a fast-track guy.
He was maybe even a little crazy."

Forget about flextime, the man of the 1990s, TV commer-
cials with glowing dads clasping beaming babies to their
muscled chests, or any of that new-man propaganda. The
reality is that we aren't even close to accepting, let alone ap-
plauding, a man who chooses to put his children first. In
America today, a man almost always has one choice, and one
choice only: his job or his kids.

In 1991 Catalyst, a business research group, found that 63
percent of businesses surveyed didn't believe in parental
leave for fathers. And the vast majority of the firms that did
allow dads to take off when their kids were born called it
"personal leave" and didn't promote the fact that it was
available to new fathers. In 1992 *Child* magazine started track-
ing "father-friendly" companies but was forced to cancel the
effort after only one year. It couldn't find enough companies
that qualified.

Corporations may make rules and governments may make
laws, but attitudes are hard to change. You can break away
an hour early to attend your daughter's Little League game
now and then, or come in a half-hour late once in a blue
moon if you have to take your son to school, but any real
commitment to parenting will cost you on the job. It might
even cost you the job itself.

One summer Alex came to the office with me every Friday

morning for a few minutes before I took him to camp. Everybody loved him, he got to act like a big shot, and we all looked forward to Friday morning. No client was ever embarrassed by Alex and no job was ever left undone because my kid had stopped by to say hello.

But the executive who ran my division, a thin-lipped fifty-something ex–vice president of General Motors, didn't have any children of his own and didn't seem to like anybody else's much. The guy would actually grimace whenever he saw Alex in the office. One day Alex had a fever and his mom was on deadline and couldn't break away. I was also on deadline and had to be in the office, but we had run out of alternatives. Alex couldn't go to school, so I took him to work with me. He was well-behaved and stayed in my office most of the time. Nevertheless, the next day I was told by my supervisor that our boss, the executive with the thin lips, didn't want Alex in the office anymore. It was very clear that this was an order, not a negotiable request.

I gave notice a few weeks later.

Unless you're fortunate enough to be the boss yourself, own your own business, or work for one of those rare firms with parent-friendly policies that extend to fathers, you're probably going to have to sacrifice your career for your children. If you live near your kids, you'll have to decline the promotion that would mean moving to another city. You won't work the weekend of that big presentation because it's your boy's birthday party. Or you'll come in an hour late and get docked in pay because your little girl woke up with strep throat and had to go to the doctor right away. You might be passed up for advancement because you haven't demonstrated that you're "part of the team."

This may sound like a sacrifice, and maybe it is. But for divorced dads, who don't get to come home to our kids every night, there is no gray area on the subject of sacrifice. *Your kids are more important than your job.* It's that simple. If you don't feel that way, or if you do but are unable or unwilling to put the belief into practice, you'll have trouble making divorced parenting work. You'll be as much a stranger to your kids as workaholics in nuclear families are to their children.

Long before he became one of the top executives of a fathers' rights organization, Joseph McMillen learned that nothing a person does is more important than being a parent. To pay his way through college, young Joseph worked in hospices and nursing homes, helping people "pass from one side of life to another," as he describes it. Not once during the years he spent ministering to the terminally ill did he hear someone on his deathbed bemoan a business deal that didn't happen or a football play that didn't get made. Their only regret, people would tell him in their final moments, was that they didn't spend enough time with their kids.

When it comes to spending time with your kids, it's real hard to do if you live halfway across the country.

Don't Go the Distance

In 1987–1988 the National Survey of Families and Households found that 14 percent of all fathers reported having a child who did not live with them at least half the time. More than one out of four of these "absentee" dads had seen their kids less than once a month in the previous twelve months, and 21 percent hadn't seen them at all.

The children of the fathers in those groups were undeniably "at risk" because of their fathers' absence, emotionally as well as physically. Distance is one of a divorced dad's greatest enemies. In terms of your child's emotional health, keeping your distance is one of the worst decisions you can make as a divorced dad.

Advertising executive Art Edelstein never put down his ex-wife in front of his son, not even after he remarried. They lived in Chicago and she lived in California, and Art's son would go to the Coast at prearranged times every year to spend some time with his mother. When his son was about sixteen years old, Art made visiting his ex-wife an option. His boy decided not to go.

The young man didn't really know his mother; he felt estranged from her. Art realized you just can't have a tight relationship with someone you only see two or three weeks a year, whether it's your mother or your father. The deadly effect of distance on parent-child relationships knows no gender.

Teachers, psychologists, and other child-rearing experts know how critical your physical presence is to your kids' well-being, and they will let you know about it in no uncertain terms.

One noncustodial dad and his ex-wife worked fairly well at co-parenting their young son. When the boy began having some trouble at school, both parents met with his teacher after class to design a plan of action to get him back on the right track.

The boy's father mentioned that he and his ex-wife were not getting along well, and in fact had been arguing just that week because he thought—wrongly—that she had been planning to move out of state. They all laughed at the miscommunication; then the teacher looked both parents right in the eyes and said, softly but firmly, "Whatever you do, don't go anywhere for the next year."

Your child needs *you*, not just your voice on the phone or a letter in the mail every week. Your ex-wife, whether she acknowledges it or not, needs you too, to help her raise your kid. And don't settle for being what online fathers' rights crusader Dean Hughson calls a "Days Inn Dad," someone who occasionally flies, drives, or takes the train to his ex-wife's town to snatch hurried chunks of time with his kids in lonely hotel rooms.

That's not what your children need you to be. They need you to be a teacher, an authority figure, a protector, and yes, a friend. Without enough face-to-face contact, you can't be those things. If it is at all within your power, *do not live far away from your children.*

At times you may have to battle the urge to do otherwise. Literally and figuratively running away from a broken family seems to be some sort of perverse instinct in many divorced men. Two weeks after my breakup, I called my father on the East Coast and broke down, crying, "I want to come home." I didn't, of course. In fact, my wife and I had moved to California expressly to get away from New York. But the agony of a divorce brings out the male flight impulse. Go away, a tiny voice in your head says, over and over. Go anywhere else but here.

Don't listen.

While visiting a parenting chat room in cyberspace, I read a particularly poignant plea for advice from a divorced dad who was yearning to return to his hometown to start over. He and his ex were splitting parenting duties fifty-fifty, and his three-year-old daughter seemed to be doing well, but he was hoping, down the road a bit, to be able to return to the town where he had been born. He was looking for creative solutions to this long-distance parenting problem.

"I feel like I'm really trapped," he wrote. "I need to do what's best for me, but I also believe strongly that I need to be there for my daughter. Plus I very much enjoy being a dad. HELP!!"

He received only one truly coherent reply, but it was a good one. The respondent was a divorced dad himself, and had always lived close to his daughter until her mother remarried and moved to Seattle. Despite a legal battle, the court let her take the daughter and move, but they cut this father's child support payments so that he could make regular visits to see his child—which he did, every month for a year and a half. Eventually the father remarried and the mother moved back from Seattle. The young girl lives about three miles from her dad, and he's happy to have her back home.

What he said to the cyberspace dad with the dilemma was this: "A daughter needs her father, and you can't be a father from so far away. She is just too young to be juggling two lives, and that is just too much to ask of her. I know you have your life and that you need to 'start over,' but you have a little girl who needs you, whom you helped bring into this world, and whom you are responsible for. Stay with that little girl. She needs both parents close to her."

Well said. I don't know what this divorcing dad ultimately decided, but from the description of his relationship with his wife, he has a solid basis for cooperation. For his little girl's sake, I hope he stayed close by.

Sometimes distancing yourself from your kids can't be helped, of course, because you're not the one in motion. As in the previous example, *she* does the moving. In that case, you should demand (and you are legally entitled) to have your kids all summer, during Christmas recess, on other holidays like Father's Day, and on your birthday. Plus you should make a point of arranging to be with your kid one or two other times during the year, when it isn't holiday season and you can spend some everyday time with each other.

The Disappearing Dad

Tom, a program designer, had an ex-wife who gleefully told their two young boys about dreams she had in which she killed their father. She also regularly told them their dad was an "airhead" and the divorce was all their father's fault. The older boy, now nine, has had numerous emotional problems and is currently under a therapist's care. His brother, two years younger, also demonstrates a great deal of confusion over his parents' divorce and is developing emotional problems of his own.

What happened to Tom is the collective nightmare of every divorced dad. It's called "parentectomy" by family therapist Dr. Frank Williams of Cedars Sinai Hospital in Los Angeles, and "Parental Alienation Syndrome" in its most virulent form by the acclaimed child psychiatrist Richard Gardner, author of two seminal books on the effects of divorce, *The Boys and Girls Book About Divorce* and *The Parents Book About*

Divorce. Parentectomy occurs when a custodial parent tries to alienate the noncustodial parent from the children. Parent Alienation Syndrome is the most extreme form of the tactic, when the custodial parent attempts to completely remove the other parent from the kids' lives.

If you're a divorced dad, chances are you've encountered at least a mild form of this lovely behavior. Even in nuclear families, many mothers exhibit a possessive "gatekeeper" attitude about their children. They determine when and how much time the father sees the children, and they pass continual and often severe judgment on Dad's ability to parent if his style conflicts with theirs—which it always does to some degree. The tendency can be even more pronounced, of course, if the mother is divorced and has custody of the children. This is especially so if there are arguments over money, because some custodial mothers threaten to withhold visitation rights unless Dad pays up.

Continual badmouthing of the noncustodial parent can be a form of parentectomy. Denial of visitation, obviously, is unambiguous parentectomy, a direct attempt to reduce or extinguish a father's relationship with his children. Sometimes the noncustodial parent will respond to attempts to block access to his children with renewed rage and hostility, and then both parents fight viciously, usually in front of the kids. You can guess who suffers most in that scenario.

At its worst, parentectomy can force a noncustodial parent to give up and remove himself from his children's lives. As I said earlier, most of us divorced dads at one time or another have felt that deadly urge to give up, go away, let our children go on without us. Sometimes it just hurts too much to keep on fighting, especially when your little ones start repeating their mother's criticisms of you almost verbatim.

Nothing is more catastrophic to the children of divorce than having one parent removed from their lives. Kids have a tendency to blame the noncustodial parent anyway, since he or she (usually Dad) is the one who "left," but that's just surface bravado. Underneath, kids blame themselves for the departure, believing that they failed in some way to be good enough for the parent to stay. Not at all incidentally, and even less surprisingly, a parent forced to take himself out of his kids' lives also is far less likely to be willing to pay child support.

No wonder Dr. Williams calls parentectomy "psychologically lethal" to children. Kids whose noncustodial parents have been ripped out of their lives often have deep emotional problems later on, and some even become suicidal.

By the way, parentectomy is not committed only by ex-wives. A child's grandparents can be just as bad and sometimes worse. Time and time again, I have seen instances when the grandparents have relentlessly and with extraordinary cruelty tried to shove a divorced dad out of their grandchildren's lives. Appeals for peace for the benefit of the child fall on stone-deaf ears, because the grandparents' hostility usually is the rock-hard product of out-of-control parental protectiveness.

A single dad named Shane recently was forced into a bitter and costly legal battle to keep his daughter's mother from changing the girl's last name—because the *parents* of her new husband, demanding that the child treat them as grandparents, provoked the attempted name change. Shane is still combating the reverberations from this ugly attempt at parentectomy. During a walk on the beach (a tradition when she's at her daddy's house), his little girl brought up the subject of a name change again, expressing some unusually mature observations on the subject for a five year-old. Startled and suspicious, Shane asked his daughter why she was bringing it up again. She said her grandparents told her to.

Most fathers don't face situations as severe as the ones Shane and Tom had to deal with, but every good man must be vigilant about the potential for parentectomy, and honest about his own reactions to it. If your ex attempts to influence how your kids think of you, consistently denies you access to them, or actively seeks to undermine your relationship with your children, try to make her understand how much she's hurting *them* by her actions. If that attempt fails and the effort to drive a wedge between you and your kids continues or intensifies, *run* to the best lawyer you can find and sue for joint physical custody. Today's family law courts will often be sympathetic to your plea if you can show even a minimal involvement and interest in your young ones' lives.

That's what Tom did.

And he won.

More Tips for Good Men

Whether your kids live near or far, whether or not you've got an ex-wife who is cooperative, here are some other tips for staying involved that you may find useful. These are drawn from my own experience and from the experiences of other dads, as well as from a company called Familyware, a Florida shareware provider that focuses on noncustodial parenting:

• *Call your kids at least once a week.* This is extra important if you live far away. And make it a consistent dad ritual by calling on the same day and at the same time every week. You want your children to look forward to your call. Make sure you choose a time when both you and your kids can talk for a while without being rushed.

• *Send your children a book that they can read to you during your phone conversations.* If the book is a long one, they can read a chapter at a time. Or, during one of their visits, take them shopping, and pick out a children's book of poetry together. Read the book together while your children are with you, and pick out a favorite poem. They can then read the poem to you over the phone. The pilgrimage to the mall to buy the book will be an indelible memory in your mutual history with your children.

• *Install a special phone line for your little one.* When business-man Jeff's ex began dating again, she would let the answer-ing machine pick up while she was having wine and dinner with her dates. Jeff got tired talking to the machine even though he knew his son was there, so he called the phone company and for $50 had a line installed in his son Billy's bedroom. Only Jeff and Billy's aunt have the number. So when the phone rings, Billy knows it's for him.

"I call almost every day," says Jeff. "Sometimes we talk for half an hour, sometimes for only twenty seconds. I would recommend it for any divorced dad, especially if your child is really young."

• *Buy something enduring that symbolizes the bond between you and your children.* When your children visit, go shopping to-gether and pick out a rose bush or some flowering plant. Let them help you plant it and take care of it during their stay with you. Then, over the years, you can watch it grow to-gether. When your children return to their mother's home, snip a flower off the plant and send it to them. They will conjure up your presence every time they smell that flower's bouquet. Or take pictures of it every so often to let them know it's thriving. If you don't have a backyard, cut a potato in half, secure half of it with toothpicks, and stick the other half in a jar of water. It will eventually start growing into a plant. You'll still be able to share the pleasure of watching something grow.

• *Ask to be placed on your kids' school mailing list.* And when you learn that special activities are taking place, arrange to send cupcakes or whatever is appropriate at that time. This way, your young "Peter Pan," starting quarterback, or drum-mer in the school band has a tangible reminder that although you couldn't be there in the flesh, you were there in spirit.

• *Buy your children useful things with their names on them.* Make sure you're the one who buys at least a portion of your children's school supplies, for example, and include "special" pencils with their names on them. You might even send special imprinted chairs or monogrammed towels and washcloths. Each time your children use these, they'll think of you.

• *Keep photographic record of your mutual history.* Don't send photographs or videos with just you in them. Make sure your little ones also get pictures of your dog that they love so much, and the trip you took together. And make them large: eight-by-ten blowups in living color. Or order duplicates of all the photos you send, and place them in a special photo album just for your children. I've done this with Alex, and I have a photo wall in my place as well. He never tires of looking at either, and will often point to someone or someplace and say who or what it is. What he's doing is making sure he remembers his history. Pocket-sized photo albums also make great gifts for your kids.

Being involved takes a little more work when you're a divorced dad, but the payoffs are tremendous. Of course, it's easier to stay involved when you and your ex are cooperative. In the next chapter, I'll give you some suggestions on how to form a parenting team with your ex that will ensure that you both play a big part in your kids' life.

CHAPTER 5

❖

Divided We Stand:
Co-parenting Golden Rules

The only California Condor egg known to have been
laid this season was knocked off a cliff by the parents who were fighting. A team of specialists trying
to save the huge, endangered birds watched from
half a mile as the four-inch egg smashed on the
rocks below the condor's cave, and the embryo was
eaten by ravens. The condors, the specialists said,
were battling over which of them should take care
of the egg.

—UNITED PRESS INTERNATIONAL

Articles written by scientists in scientific journals are usually
so dry you could use them for kindling. The above passage,
however, is the most visceral metaphor for America's uncivil
war that I've ever read. Whenever I hear divorced parents

snarling about their miserable ex-spouses (and I hear it all the time), I tell them the story of those tragically foolish condors and their poor smashed egg.

It gets their attention.

You may have no difficulty understanding intellectually that you have to work with your ex-wife for the benefit of your kids. In practice, however, it's emotional torture trying to make co-parenting work. Divorced dads are usually at a disadvantage from the beginning; in most states, the custodial parent holds all the cards. Plus, of course, you are buffeted back and forth by the hostility, petty vengeance, and sniping that always goes on between two divorced people.

As a divorced dad, you've heard the cliché at least a thousand times: even though the marriage is over, you and your former mate remain linked because of your kids. But how do you keep the tie that still binds you to her from strangling the rest of your life? It isn't easy and it's often unfair, but you can make it work.

Joint physical custody is enthusiastically heralded by fathers' rights activists because it makes explicit what the concept of in the "best interest of the child" implies: the ideal parenting solution is one that includes both the mother and the father. Joint physical custody gives that concept the force of law. More and more fathers are pressing for full family rights, declaring that in many instances they can do as good a job of rearing their kids as their ex-wives do. And more and more judges are agreeing.

As I've noted, the postdivorce parenting cake can be sliced in an infinite number of ways. Veteran divorce lawyer Henry Gornbein, president of the American Divorce Information Network, has written about or helped construct joint arrangements that ranged from parents living within blocks of each other so the kids can drift back and forth, to highly organized custody "schemata," as Gornbein calls them, where physical custody shifts from one parent to the other every four months.

It's true, joint physical custody is a fashionable legal device. But the idea that mothers and fathers *have* to, *ought* to, even *must* work together for the benefit of their kids isn't limited to couples whose postdivorce cooperation is formally blessed by law. Fathers with joint legal custody also are partners with their ex-wives in parenting. Many sundered couples with no legal recognition of their mutual importance to the family also share parenting duties and time with their kids.

Anecdotal evidence is strong that shared "parenting time" is more common than evidenced by court records. Gornbein estimates that for every couple that returns to court after their divorce to renegotiate custody, there are sixty or seventy others who have worked out a system on their own. Only about 10 percent of the divorced dads interviewed for this book have joint physical custody, but a solid majority of them have shared parenting arrangements with their ex-wives that go beyond what the conventional visitation schedule usually allows, or at least beyond what their particular divorce settlement stipulates. These fathers have their kids—or at least have access to them—around 30 percent of the time or more.

From what the research shows, from what the experts say, and, most important, from what divorced dads experience, it's clear that three things are essential for effective co-parenting. These three form a firm tripod upon which divorced dads should base their postdivorce parenting strategy.

The Co-parenting Tripod

1. Minimize conflict with your ex-wife.
2. Minimize contact with your ex-wife.
3. Maximize access to and visitation with your children.

Number one is the be-all and end-all of divorced parenting, and one I've mentioned already: the less conflict you have with your ex-wife, the better your relationship with your kids will be. We've already seen some specific examples of that dynamic in action. We'll see more in the chapters to come.

Number two, naturally, is affected by the amount of co-operating you do. The more you share parenting, the more you will be forced to communicate and work with your former wife. That's okay, as long as you remember to keep contact to the bare minimum necessary to do business. Greg, whom we met earlier, has asked that his wife contact him only at his office, not at home. Unless, of course, there's an emergency.

The final leg of the tripod is right up there with conflict on the divorced-dad affect-o-meter. The more contact you have with your kids, the closer your relationship with them will be.

With the Co-parenting Tripod, you can construct a system for coexistence with your former beloved and a philosophical framework for your divorced-dad parenting style. To execute your strategy, you need tactics. Many different techniques for shared parenting have been investigated by divorce researchers and recommended by psychologists and sociologists, but they can be summarized in ten rules. By adhering as strictly as possible to these simple but effective tactics within the framework of the tripod, you can make a go of being a divorced dad. I call them the Golden Rules of Co-parenting.

Golden Rule #1: Approach Postdivorce Parenting as Uncharted Territory

You know that patronizing look veteran parents give first-timers when the rookies are in a panic over an incident of projectile vomiting, a fight on the tetherball court during recess, or some other commonplace kid rite of passage? Give it to yourself in the mirror every time you feel like you've just scarred your kid for life because you committed some minor and universal divorced-dad error.

The last thing you should do is be even harder on yourself

than everybody else is. The confusion over what divorce studies actually say about the consequences of a sundered marriage should have tipped you off—*there is no formula for surviving life after divorce.* Divorce has been around forever, but nobody really paid any attention to it until the past decade or so. It's a brand-new field for the so-called experts and for you.

Beginning a chapter on shared parenting by telling you, in effect, to think of yourself first has a certain irony, I'll agree. But if you're making yourself crazy over what to do and how to do it, you're probably also driving you ex-wife mad. Not a good idea when you're trying to forge a strong co-parenting team.

Which brings up another area of the uncharted territory you'll want to explore. If you're like most people, you've probably never studied communication, conflict resolution, or negotiation—unless it's part of your job. But if you want to learn to cooperate, you've got to understand the dynamics of those three skills. Some divorced dads even take "how to negotiate" classes to help them deal more effectively with their ex-wives. You'd be surprised how often those classes help. Make yourself a student of the general concepts of cooperation. And check into various self-help groups—many offer courses that can help you learn vital divorced-dad skills to deal with conflict resolution and negotiating.

But don't depend totally on classes and experts. Listen to yourself too. You'll find that your most fruitful divorced-dad parenting moments are often unplanned—and sometimes unrecognized. Most of us have some fairly reliable ideas on what we shouldn't do in divorced parenting, but when it comes to what we should do, all we have to go on are some general guidelines, the experiences of those who have come before us, and our own gut instincts. Listen to that voice; it's apt to be pretty reliable. You can do all the right things, read all the right books, but in the end, what feels right for you is what's going to be right for you.

So don't beat yourself up over your parenting. We're all just as confused as you are.

Golden Rule #2: Practice Patience

Nobody makes decisions in a vacuum. We're all susceptible to bad advice from well-meaning friends. One of the first things counselor Gwen Olitsky does when she starts working with divorced or divorcing men is to advise them to be patient until their ex-wives get out from under the shadow of their female "network." Much of the nastiness divorced fathers receive right after our marriages break up, especially when we try to be conciliatory, is from the good-old-girl networks that most women have—girlfriends, sisters, mothers.

A newly divorced woman is vulnerable and feeling very much the victim. Chances are, she's getting all sorts of vindictive counsel from her circle of female advisers countering your attempts to co-parent, mostly along the lines of "oh sure, he says that now, but honey, we've been there and they're all rotten. Go get a killer lawyer and nail the bum."

The only way to handle this is to wait out the storm. Stop trying to convince her of what a nice guy you are; you never will. Tell her what you believe simply and honestly. If it's your truth, that's a different internal dynamic than trying to play the noble hero, and you'll be able to withstand the storm of vituperation. And keep telling yourself why you're doing all this in the first place—for your kids, because it's the right thing to do.

Most ex-wives will come around eventually, especially if you keep your word, don't spring any nasty surprises, and refuse to be drawn into games of insult Ping-Pong. Understand where she's coming from and hang tough. And with your kids, just say, "You know, sometimes your mother does stuff I don't agree with. That's okay. There are two sides to every story. She has hers; I have mine." There's nothing wrong with teaching your kid about the inevitability of multiple points of view. And remember your omnipresent role as teacher—if you counter wild accusations and unfair criticism with humor, equanimity, and grace, you are teaching your children a valuable lesson about how to handle life.

Golden Rule #3: Choose Your Counsel Wisely

During your divorce and probably for at least a year or two after it, you are going to need the advice of counsel. You may even retain your divorce lawyer for years after that, if additional court contests become necessary. Whatever the case, *don't get a "killer lawyer."* Please. Trust me on this. Beyond the fact that such attorneys are usually extremely unpleasant human beings, remember that what you have gotten yourself into isn't a holy crusade against the Devil cleverly disguised as your former spouse. It's an uncivil war between two scarred and confused humans, and the real losers are your kids. Get a lawyer who gives a damn, who, when you want to indulge some petty revenge idea, will remind you that none of this is a game to your children, not some shyster who'll take your money and run back into court.

Your divorce isn't the trial of the century. Get an attorney who will listen to you and whose impulse is always toward peace, not war—someone who understands that courts shouldn't play dice with children's lives.

Golden Rule #4: Set Some Rules—Then Play by Them

Each couple has its own way of settling things. Nobody disagrees on everything all the time in a marriage, so divorced couples have at least a few examples of times when they were able to work something out.

Take those examples and use them as building blocks to *craft a postdivorce negotiating agreement:* how you and she will resolve parenting issues. Then stick to the agreement. Acknowledge that you have different points of view. There will be times when you disagree, but have a specific framework within which you talk it out and come to a resolution. Make sure to include provisions for those times when you're not making progress, or negotiations may degenerate into name-calling and tantrum-throwing.

For instance, my ex-wife and I often fight when we talk by telephone. So we have agreed on a phone negotiating system (verbal and implicit, not written and explicit, but the principle is the same) that has worked well for more than five years. Whenever one of us is getting annoyed or angered by what the other one is saying (or, more frequently, how the other one is saying it), we don't try to get the other one to stop. We know from bitter experience that there's little chance of that happening. So the one becoming annoyed simply says, "I can't talk to you now. Good-bye." If the subject needs to be addressed right away, we might wait only a few minutes before talking again. If it's a subject that isn't pressing, we'll discuss it some other time.

It works. Neither she nor I is offended when the other one does that. And the next time we talk, we're back to being polite and businesslike with each other—and whatever we'd been talking about gets resolved.

When crafting your agreement, agree to try it out for a short time, then rethink the formula and try for a while longer. Then review it again several months later. This way, events won't overtake your ability to cooperate.

I wholeheartedly agree with some states, scores of therapists, and successful divorced dads who believe that the more formal you make these agreements, the better off you and your children will be. So *draw up a parenting plan, a specific point-by-point blueprint for how the two of you are going to co-parent.*

Several divorce experts defer to Isolina Ricci, author of *Mom's House, Dad's House* (Collier Books, 1980), on the formation of a viable parenting plan. The mechanisms Ricci suggests that divorced couples use to cooperate are similar to many of those recommended here. Her book includes an example of a parenting plan between a fictitious couple with two preadolescent children, which details who does what, when, and with whom. I've adapted some of Ricci's suggestions and added my own comments to create a list that you can use to help you create your own plan.

• *Terminology*. Ricci's fictitious couple agrees to use pop culture psychobabble instead of legal definitions with each other and with their kids, terms like "second home parent" instead of "noncustodial parent." Although I'm a firm believer in the power of words, this kind of euphemistic language seems to me politically correct nonsense. I doubt you'll do your kids irreparable harm by using legal terms.

• *Responsibility*. Who's responsible for what? This important category affirms that both parents have a right to be involved in their kids' education, choice of pediatrician, and other important areas of their lives. So make it complete.

• *Contributions*. Spell out time contributions for each parent, as well as who pays how much in child support. This is an essential part of any co-parenting agreement.

• *Medical and dental*. Make it completely clear who will pay for what. Don't forget to include transportation responsibilities and who handles everyday medical needs—such as ear infections and scraped knees.

• *Education and child care*. Lay out where the kids will go to school. Have both parents pledge to attend teacher conferences and the like, and include a breakdown of costs—for example, Dad pays tuition, Mom pays ongoing school costs, such as money for field trips and gifts for the teacher. Be sure to include in your plan a detailed agreement on who pays for back-to-school stuff and what that includes—not just rulers and pencils, but backpacks, school clothes, and gym clothes.

• *Children's activities.* Include a breakdown of responsibility for the kids' music lessons, athletic involvement, and other activities—like Little League and gymnastics—including who will be responsible for getting them to all practices and events. Don't forget to include birthday gifts for friends; those costs can add up quickly.

• *Respect for one another's parenting style and authority.* This is a vital category for divorced dads. Each parent should promise to respect the other's parenting style and to encourage the kids to talk to each parent honestly about problems. Don't forget to include a provision stating that discipline and house rules will be jointly enforced and that badmouthing by either parent of the other one is taboo.

• *Agreement time period and renegotiations for new agreement.* I agree with Ricci's suggested two years, with automatic renewal at the end of that time if no revisions are necessary. Should one parent wish to revise the agreement before the two years are up, the couple might agree to negotiate for a month before going into court, if necessary, to resolve the issues.

The Children's Rights Council (CRC) also provides some helpful tips in *The Best Parent Is Both Parents*, its shared parenting guide. The guide is designed to be used as a premarital agreement to minimize the risk of divorce, but the information can be adapted slightly, as I've done here, to help divorced parents as well.

The CRC advises parents to ask themselves a series of questions before crafting a parenting (or divorced parenting) plan. Inability to agree on the answers to many of these questions may be the very reasons you and your ex-wife were divorced, because they concern your values and parenting styles.

If you can work on this with your ex, you will be way ahead in the divorced-dad game. Simply talking about these issues with your ex-wife may help you avoid a long and sorry laundry list of problems and conflicts down the road. The questions include:

• How do you define [postdivorce] parenting? Does it include emotional support, providing a role model, taking care of the child's daily needs and economic support? Or is parenting more than that?

• What form of discipline do you believe in—guidance and positive setting of limits, punishment, or providing an example? Would you allow corporal punishment by your spouse, school or others? [Do you believe the two of you should have a postdivorce discipline system you both follow?]

• What of the importance of play for a child? Should play be cultivated and encouraged? Do you both agree to provide your children [postdivorce] with activities in the fields of music, art, dance and sports? [Where will such classes be taken and who will pay for them?]

• What about religion? Do you agree on one faith? If not, which faith will your children be raised in?

• What values do you wish to impart to the children regarding honesty, work, family and friends? [When, and by whom, will the children be told about drugs, sex, and teen pregnancy?]

• Will each of you respect the other parent as important to the child?

• How much time should each of you spend with your child, in keeping with other responsibilities?

• If your child has emotional or learning problems, would you be willing to admit a problem exists? Would you be willing or reluctant to seek professional help for those problems? [Would you be willing to go

together to a therapist postdivorce for the purpose of helping your child, and who will pay for such sessions?]
- What role should grandparents or other relatives play in your children's lives [postdivorce]?

Golden Rule #5: Keep Your Cool

"The problem with divorce," says feminist Karen DeCrow, "is that grown-ups don't act grown up."

Tell me about it. If the mirror in my bedroom recorded on film what it reflected, the film would show a red-faced Mr. Feuer, eyes ablaze, screaming on an almost daily basis about some inhuman wrong done him by the former Mrs. Feuer. I've yelled at that innocent mirror louder and more often than a Marine drill sergeant roars at his recruits. But I always try not to do it in my ex-wife's presence, and especially not in front of Alex.

One of the most important Golden Rules of Co-parenting is: *control your anger.* Easier said then done, I know, but you have to do it. Period. Even with your ex-wife. Follow the advice of Melinda Blau, author of the excellent divorce book *Families Apart,* who says you should "become really big when you're angry."

As I've mentioned before, the degree of conflict among divorced parents is by far the strongest indicator of whether their children will have problems later on, and naturally the degree of conflict rises or falls with the level of anger between you and your ex, what shrinks like to call "emotional charge." You can take some comfort in the probability that sooner or later, you're both likely to calm down: according to one study on the subject, 85 percent of divorced parents were no longer very hostile eighteen months after they were divorced. In the meantime, however, you must control the immediate urge to get even.

Remember, the biggest psychological problem you're likely to have to address with your kids is the almost inevitable belief on their part that they're somehow responsible for the divorce. When you fight with your ex-wife in front of them, you're just feeding that belief. If you insult her, you're telling your kids that one half of them is no good.

So don't do it. Just say no to your temper. When I find myself yelling at my ex in front of my son (it happens; don't expect to be perfect), I analyze why I flew off the handle, and if I'm clearly in the wrong, I make a point of apologizing to my ex in front of my son. Even if I'm right, I get eye-level with Alex and let him know in no uncertain terms that Mommy and Daddy were not fighting because of him.

I'm not suggesting you meekly submit if your ex is verbally reaming you out, but there are better, less harmful ways of handling these situations than lobbing insults at each other. One way is to try to reason with her. Whatever you may be thinking, don't use incendiary words and phrases. Let's face it, we're no angels, and most ex-wives aren't really High Priestesses of the Bitch Clan, either, even though we divorced dads may feel they act like it sometimes. Still, if you can convince your ex that word-whipping you in front of your children is not in the kids' best interests, she'll back off.

Linda Napolitano, president of the single-parent social organization Parents Without Partners, believes a significant reason that she and her ex-husband have been able to successfully co-parent (they've been divorced for fifteen years) is that she doesn't belittle him in front of their daughter. (A second big reason probably is that her ex-husband helps with discipline, a Golden Rule we'll explore later on in this chapter.)

Another method to handle your ex-wife's attempts to push your buttons until you scream is to remind yourself constantly that you don't live with her anymore. This one really works for me. Like most divorced men, I am no longer in a figurative shooting war with my former true love, but a potential argument is always bubbling not far below the surface. Civilized discourse may not convince her to change her behavior, but I can certainly control what I say or do. If Alex isn't present or the badmouthing takes the form of low-level goading that annoys me but doesn't set me off like a firecracker on the Fourth of July, I keep telling myself that this is no longer a marriage, where you literally have to sleep with the enemy. I can walk away.

So hold your tongue and keep the peace for fifteen minutes, an hour, or even an afternoon, however long you must stay.

The head doctors recommend another method that a lot of divorced fathers use to handle their anger: *be assertive but use bargaining methods instead of anger*. This is a valuable tip—your ex-wife is an adversary you're going to be dealing with for a long, long time. If you've ever had any therapy, you'll recognize the technique. Here's how Ohio psychologist Dr. Israel Lichtenstein, one of the nation's foremost experts on divorce mediation, explains it:

"When I have a divorced father in front of me with a lot of anger, I ask him, 'Have there been any instances when your ex did something you felt was unfair and you didn't get enraged?' He'll usually think back, and say something like, 'I just laughed it off. I didn't argue. Usually, I just scream back and hang up the phone.' At that point, I ask the man what he did instead, and he'll say, 'Well, I just said I was sorry she felt that way.'

"Then the man sees that he chose to say that instead of the usual 'you stupid bitch.' Then I ask him what he was thinking of at that time that prevented him from saying 'you stupid bitch.' He may say, 'I was going out later that evening and I didn't want to be in a bad mood.' I say, 'Great, that's a wonderful accomplishment. What other times have you succeeded in creating calm moods?' And of course, I point out, anything he's done before he can do again. For example, there's the upcoming phone call tomorrow with the ex. How would he like to handle it?''

Golden Rule #6: Be Available

Make it easy for your ex to let you see your child. If your kid is sick, offer to take him to the doctor. If your ex has a critical business meeting first thing in the morning, suggest that you take your child to school. If baby-sitting isn't a right you've included in your divorce agreement, make a point of taking on that duty if you're asked, and suggest the idea if you're not.

These situations occur all the time, and if you are there, not pressing, just making yourself available as an option, you will be able to broaden your access. Indeed, it can have lasting results.

In Chapter One, I mentioned that my son stays over at my place every Thursday night. Here's how that tradition began. My marriage settlement agreement is the basic visitation scenario in which Alex stays with me every other weekend and for three hours one night a week. The night is the usual one given to ex-hubbies, Wednesday—America's Visitation Night. But about a year following our divorce, after I baby-sat on several occasions and my ex-wife was reasonably certain I wouldn't grab my kid and head for Mexico, or let him jump off the roof, I suggested that we switch my weekday night to Thursdays.

Since I live less than twenty minutes away, I also floated the idea that I keep Alex overnight every Thursday and take him to school the next morning. This gave my ex-wife a regular night off every week without having to worry about finding a sitter (or paying for one), and on one of the prime socializing nights for singles to boot. She agreed instantly, and ever since, I have had an extra night with my boy every week—a true win-win co-parenting success story.

Some custodial mothers and certain psychologists express reservations about letting a child stay at a noncustodial parent's house overnight during the week because it might confuse very young children. They also argue that overnights during the week contribute to a divorced kid's sense of instability. I have found no research to suggest that this is so, and none of the divorced dads interviewed for this book seemed to have any real problems with their children that were in any way linked to the kids' staying over at Dad's place on a weeknight.

In my case, I agreed to make explicitly sure that our son understands his mother's home is his home. He's always welcome at Daddy's house, but he lives with his mom. Everyone is happy with this arrangement, and no one is the slightest bit confused.

The point is, your desire to remain close to your children is the one area where your ex-wife's self-interest and yours should clearly and unambiguously coincide, unless she's totally deranged. Assuming that the two of you are not actively hostile to each other, you should be able to make a compelling case for this kind of expanded access to your kid.

Golden Rule #7: It's Nothing Personal

The divorced parenting-as-job metaphor is often used by experts and nonmarried parents alike as a workable way to look at your relationship with your former spouse. Coparenting is, indeed, "just like your job," says one custodial mom. "You have to know which days you have to be there, what times, and what days you have off. You can always switch a holiday or a weekend or cover for each other when one is on vacation. But you have to have the groundwork laid out."

The best relationship to have with your ex-wife is a civil and businesslike one, what divorce expert Constance Ahrons calls a "limited partnership." This is especially important, of course, if you and your ex-wife have a hard time communicating without getting tense.

Joseph McMillen, assistant operations director for the National Congress for Fathers and Children, a national organization that helps noncustodial parents maintain relationships with their kids, suggests that a divorced dad treat the mother of his children as his most important business partner. That's good advice. We all have been forced to work with people we don't like at one time or another, so we know it can be done.

Another good suggestion every divorced father should follow: *leave a paper trail of everything you've negotiated and everything you've agreed on.* If you can't, make sure some neutral third party—a teacher, a mutual friend, a therapist—witnesses the agreement. In effect, you are protecting yourself the same way you do in the business world, only there it is with memos and formal business letters. (You'll find that there are a lot of "write it down" suggestions in this book. That's not by accident. You'd be surprised how much putting pen to paper or keystroke to screen helps keep your relationship with your ex right where you want it—devoid of unpleasant surprises.)

Speaking of business letters, when you communicate with your ex this way, make very, very sure there are no negative emotions conveyed by your words, nothing that could possibly be construed as derogatory to her or anything she says or does. Too many arguments begin innocently, because one party wasn't careful enough to compose what he or she was saying or writing beforehand. Imagine that the letter is going to someone you want to joint venture with or partner up with somehow. The last thing you want to do is make her angry.

The best way to guard against this is to have a female friend give your letter the once-over. If it gets her mad, it will get your ex mad. Have her suggest alternative wording or approaches. Keep using her as a letter censor until you're confident enough that you can craft a piece of communication to your ex-wife that she won't find irritating.

When you must meet face-to-face with your ex, divorce etiquette will dictate how the two of you should relate to each other. If you and she are getting along, by all means pick up and drop off your children at her house. Some parenting experts even encourage the custodial mom to drop off her kids at their dad's house in divorced families with minimum or no conflict. For most of us, however, that is unfortunately not an option.

If you and your former wife are still in conflict, or you normally get along more or less okay but at the moment you are having some conflict, the "minimal contact" part of the tripod becomes critical. Let's say you pick up your kids at their mother's house on Friday and return them there on Sunday. Likewise for your Wednesday night visitation. Those are four potentially volatile meetings that need not occur.

Maybe you can arrange to pick up your kids directly from school on Fridays and take them to school on Monday morning. During your weekly visitation period, you can keep your children overnight and drive them to school the next morning, as I do with my son. Or perhaps you should consider neutral ground, another concept you can borrow from the business world.

Neutral ground is where many important business negotiations take place, and your postdivorce relationship with your former spouse is, in effect, one very long negotiation. Neutral ground is anywhere neither you nor your ex-wife feels threatened. The divorced parents in the 1995 movie *Bye Bye Love* picked up and dropped off their kids at the local McDonald's.

In our professional lives, we don't always do business face-to-face, and the same is true of nonnuclear parenting: if you have business with your ex—you need to talk to each other to coordinate pickup or dropoff, or there's a problem with your child at school—establish prearranged phone conversations after your children go to bed. In these conversations you can discuss whatever needs to be discussed at a distance, minimizing the chance of fireworks. These are also good times to prearrange several meetings in a row.

Any successful business enterprise operates from a carefully considered plan, and you should be just as detailed with your postdivorce parenting. Divorce settlements do not automatically include clearly stated custody and visitation schedules, and divorcing couples don't always think to include them. If you don't have a detailed and precise visitation plan written into your divorce agreement, it is vital that you work out with your ex-wife when you will have your children during the week, on holidays, and during vacations, including who picks up and drops off the kids, and when. This will benefit you as the noncustodial parent tremendously, and will greatly reduce the chance of miscommunication.

Golden Rule #8: Bend, Don't Break

Bobby and his daughter live on opposite ends of the country. He sees eleven-year-old Laura at Christmas, on spring break, and in the summer . . . usually. Bobby was divorced when Laura was only two years old, and as she got older, both he and her mom realized that the original visitation agreement just didn't fit anymore. So even though Laura's mom has remained somewhat inflexible, Bobby doesn't worry if Laura misses a visit. His daughter has his number and calls him when she wants to see him, which is often.

Michael Krauss and his ex-wife began with a week-on, week-off joint custody arrangement, but it's constantly being rearranged. If one parent wants to take their two girls shopping, or spend the morning with them, the other usually has no problem. In fact, the nonnuclear Krauss/Lunden family has a postdivorce tradition: one night during their "week off," the noncustodial parent for that week takes the girls to dinner. The bottom line is that neither parent is without the kids for more than three days at a time.

Krauss's arrangement and Bobby's visitation schedule are typical—not the setups themselves, but the fact that the setups change all the time. Golden Rule #8 means *be flexible*, because in divorce, as in life itself, the only thing you can count on is that everything will change all the time.

The most detailed divorce agreements sometimes seem to lay out how you're going to spend every day of the rest of your life. You have the kids on Easter and Christmas during odd-numbered years. You get the boys the first half of spring break; you take delivery of the girls the first night of Thanksgiving when it falls on even-numbered days, and on and on. But one of the benefits of life's untidy nature is that it always screws up lawyers' plans as well as your own. There are those weekends when your ex-wife has the kids but she really wants to go to the beach with her girlfriends. So you make a temporary change in the agreement. Then there's that New Year's Eve when you're supposed to have the kids but she's got nothing to do and you've been invited to a party at the most exclusive restaurant in town. Another change. You take the kids in the former instance and she takes them in the latter. As part of the agreement to rearrange the visitation schedule, you both make sure you agree on makeup days or weekends.

Shifting visitation around is not only in everybody's self-interest, it is essential to the vast majority of us whose lives take place in the real, chaotic world. So be open to it.

Golden Rule #9: Don't Be a "Disneyland Dad"— Keep Up the Discipline

Those every-other weekends are so delicate, so special, you feel the urgency of making every get-together memorable. The time you spend with your kids is precious and painfully limited, so you're not going to waste a second. Every minute at your house is going to be fun and games, no arguments, no pain.

Major mistake.

We've talked about how badmouthing dad is the biggest complaint ex-husbands make of their ex-wives. Well, dads not sharing in the discipline is by far the biggest beef custodial moms have with their former mates.

This tendency of divorced dads to ignore discipline really irked Linda Napolitano. As the custodial parent, Linda was the disciplinarian, the one who made all the decisions about her child, especially in the early years. She made a point of saying, "Okay, this is a problem for Daddy too" and if there was a major disciplinary crisis, she would call up her ex-husband. He would come over, they would work together on the problem, and the arrangement was successful. As Linda says, "It's a package deal; nobody is the good guy or the bad guy."

Even dads who pride themselves on their ability to be disciplinarians can fall into the Disneyland Dad trap. *Your kids need you to be an authority figure* more than they need you to be a buddy.

Consistency in discipline at both parents' homes provides children of divorce with stability in their lives. This is not the same as blindly doing what your ex is doing just because she happens to think she wrote the book on perfect parenting, something you are in all probability already fighting against. It won't be fatal if your kid stays up an hour later at your house, for instance, but on the larger discipline issues it's vital that your offspring understand that their parents are on the same page.

When your child loses it at school—gets into a fight at recess, talks back to the teacher, the usual pushing-the-boundaries kid stuff—and Mom says "no videos" and it's your night, don't turn on a tape. Conversely, if the child does something on Sunday morning you feel compelled to impose punishment for, make Mom understand that the punishment should not be lifted just because the child goes back home to her on Sunday evening. Chances are she'll not only understand, but will thank you for the involvement.

Cooperating on discipline is a sign of mutual respect and a further hedge against using the kids as pawns. Even a good man like Tom, who truly has the ex-wife from hell, will not countermand a rule or punishment his boys' mother has set down, and it doesn't matter if the punishment is one Tom would have inflicted or not.

Golden Rule #10: Be a Man

Jeanette Lofas seems bemused by the fact that more men than women call up her Stepfamily Foundation hotline for advice. After twenty years of counseling parents in crisis, she's not surprised that, though men clearly need her help, most are uncomfortable talking about how their divorce has affected them. What does make her shake her head in puzzlement, even after two decades, is why they so quickly forget to be men when they are divorced or when they remarry.

Your kids need you to be a man. Why? Because men and women bring different ideas and perspectives to the parenting challenge. I think we'd all agree that men and women are inherently different. But when it comes to discussing these differences, especially when discussing roles, we're all forced to tread lightly—thanks to these politically correct times. That said, I'm going to plunge boldly forward anyway and suggest that you let your instincts take over and provide your kids with the things that you are hard-wired to do.

First of all, be upfront with them. The laconic male "here's the way it is" approach may be a cliché, but it's good to be straightforward. So level with them.

Tell your children that you are their father and will be forever. Their mom has a point of view about life, about your relationship with her, and about the divorce. And she has every right to her opinions. However, you also have your point of view, and you need your kids to listen to it (with the caveat, of course, that you say nothing disparaging about their mother).

Describe to your kids the fiduciary duty you have as their dad, explaining the legal structure that has been set up to govern your relationship with them. Tell them, "This is what I am supposed to do (pay child support, provide health insurance) and this is when I can see you (the visitation agreement)." Acknowledge that you and they may not like it, but let them know you all have to live with it. Ask them for their respect and support to help make the new family setup work.

Speaking to them this way may sound overly simple to you, but it really isn't. As a parent, you are a teacher, and teaching requires simple explanation and a lot of repetition. That's one of your main jobs, which is why the Disneyland Dad syndrome of fathers constantly entertaining their kids and buying them things to gain their favor always backfires. It's fun and they love it—they'll certainly take advantage of it—but in their hearts, it's not what they want from you. They're looking for guidance.

One way men teach their kids is by taking them into the backyard, throwing them a baseball, and saying, "Now throw it back." It's not necessary for them to get into the mechanics of throwing a baseball. If Dad happens to be an engineer, like one dad I know, he might actually give them a brief lecture about the physics of motion. But that's not required. Sometimes being a dad just means throwing the damn ball.

From Mom, children learn how to get by day to day—how to tie their shoes, look both ways when they cross the street, floss their teeth. From Dad, they need the big picture. Fathers give a moral viewpoint, a sense of the larger issues: right and wrong, honor, decency, the virtues of hard work. Men's rights activist Warren Farrell says that the amount of time a child spends with the father is one of the strongest predictors of empathy when that child becomes an adult.

Certainly these roles aren't ironclad. All single parents, custodial and noncustodial alike, by necessity have to take on the other gender's traditional roles to some extent. And there are individual differences, of course. Some moms are great at giving the big picture and some dads are just dandy at teaching kids how to tie their shoes. But in general, each parent gives the child a distinctly masculine or feminine piece of the puzzle of life.

For example, men play differently from women. They kid more, joke more. They're more into roughhousing, and—moms please take note—kids need that, especially boys. Dads teach their kids about independence and risk-taking, two vitally important links in the emotional development chain.

At the end of the school year, all the kids in Alex's preschool put on a show for their parents. Each kid chose a country to represent, dressed in the costume of the chosen land, and gave a little speech about the nation selected. Alex chose China because of his passion for martial arts. I helped him write a two-page speech, and his mother had him practice it the night before the show.

I arrived at the school just as the performance was about to begin and found my ex-wife seething. Apparently plans had changed and each child was to be allowed only two or three lines, and Alex, of course, had an entire monologue rehearsed. Livia was furious that the teachers hadn't told her about this change, and being a good mom, she was terrified that Alex would suffer a traumatic disaster on stage. She asked me to seek out my son's teacher and demand that Alex be allowed to give his entire speech, or at least negotiate some sort of resolution that would spare our little six-year-old the inevitable humiliation.

My first impulse was to do as she asked. But then I said, "Nah, let him wing it. Let's see what happens."

I wanted to see how my boy responded to the unexpected. I wanted him to meet the concept of risk up close and personal. I couldn't articulate it, I just knew this was an important lesson for Alex to learn. I was, of course, doing a classic dad thing.

Alex came on, did some karate moves, said a line or two about China being the largest nation on earth and the land that gave us fireworks and beautiful lanterns, and generally did a bang-up job. He sat down amid sustained and earnest applause.

I do believe that was my finest moment as a parent. Even my ex-wife admitted the whole thing turned out rather well.

Now that you've worked out the co-parenting details, and forged a good working team, what about when you're doing it alone? If you're a noncustodial dad (which most of us are), how do you make your child feel that your home is his home? Chapter Six has some answers.

CHAPTER 6

———————— ◆ ————————

Two Homes, One Hearth

Perhaps host and guest is really the happiest
relation for father and son.

—EVELYN WAUGH

The evening of the day that Gwen Olitsky brought her first
baby home, her husband was surprised to find his therapist
wife in tears. The baby's diaper needed changing and Gwen
was having an anxiety attack about it.

"I haven't had my diaper lesson yet," she cried.

"Well," said her husband, "it stands to reason that it goes
on the same way it comes off."

Gwen kept crying. Her husband just smiled and said, "I'll
do it."

In the middle of the night, when the baby began to bawl,
Gwen's husband changed the diapers again. In fact, he per-

formed that messy parental duty the first three nights the baby was home.

But Gwen wasn't asleep during these nocturnal changings. She was standing right outside the baby's room, she admits sheepishly, "making sure he didn't inadvertently kill the kid."

"If you do that one more time," her husband warned on the third night, "I'm not getting up anymore."

That was the first time Gwen realized that women are not as fair as they should be when it comes to their men's ability to parent.

In Chapter Three, we saw how difficult it is for divorced dads to come to terms with how they feel about the end of their marriage because they aren't built or conditioned to do that automatically. That doesn't mean, however, that they are inherently incapable of doing anything their children's mother does. Okay, except for breastfeeding.

"Now that I'm a single parent, I've had to learn how to do all of the things I didn't have time to do when I was married," muses one divorced dad with two young sons. "Packing school lunches. Getting the kids ready for school. Helping with homework . . . all the stuff my wife used to do that I took for granted."

Many of the attitudes we hold about the division of labor among parents are based on biology but that shouldn't lock you into ironclad roles. If you're like most fathers, you probably believe, at least to some degree, that there exists a mysterious sort of memory that gives women a cellular-level awareness of how to take care of the day-to-day needs of their kids. You are also likely to believe that whatever this biological secret is, you don't have it. Certainly, women may have a biological edge based on years of evolution, but any dedicated dad can catch up.

Georgia researchers Rex Forehand and Sarah Nousiainen studied adolescents in married families and concluded that mothers do the bulk of parenting, and if you think about your own experience, you'll likely agree there was a lot of child-rearing stuff you didn't do during your marriage just because you thought it was your wife's "job." Tender Years tradition relegates dads to a co-starring parenting role that provides them with considerably less opportunity to learn how to do the things that our culture has made gender-specific.

Our society deems innumerable activities relating to parenting the natural province of the mother, like cooking or preparing a baby bottle or applying cool rags to feverish foreheads. Have you, for example, thought about putting a rubber mat down on the floor of the bathtub at your place so your child won't slip and fall? (If you haven't, you might as well prepare yourself for at least one mad dash to the emergency room, because a kid falling down in the shower is as inevitable as the sun rising in the east.) A woman is conditioned from the time she gets her first doll to think of such things.

This parenting imbalance is often obscured in intact marriages, but not when Dad goes it alone. The little details that are left to the mother in nuclear families are exactly the kinds of things a divorced father with visitation privileges or joint physical custody has to learn how to do. Despite Michael Keaton's domestic heroics in the film that made him famous, American men in general and divorced dads in particular are woefully unprepared to be Mr. Mom.

Hollywood, in fact, has fed off the dumb-dad stereotype for decades. It's one of the more enduring traditions of television, of course, but family men aren't treated any better in the movies. The dad-as-dolt device is even more pronounced when the plot revolves around an unmarried father, and stands in stark contrast to the way single moms are portrayed.

Until very recently, when changes in society led to an emphasis on the bliss of the nuclear family, stories about the noble struggles of single moms were very popular. The plot always went something like this: with an iron will and an instinct that runs so deep she never has a moment's hesitation about her parenting decisions, heroic Super Mom raises her child or children to grow up straight and strong and true despite an environment of crime, poverty, and social injustice. She does all this and manages to keep the house clean to boot.

If there's only one child, it's usually a boy, and in that case there often is a subplot about him needing a father figure, which usually turns out to be his coach, who may or may not end up romancing Mom. The focus, however, is always squarely on Super Mom's full-service parenting ability. The child becomes a famous something or other, and in the last scene, buys Mom a house.

By contrast, single fathers on TV or in film are so obsessed with their work that they neglect their children, so wrapped up in their own grief if they're widowers that they're insensitive to their kids' needs, or just well-meaning but comically inept at parenting. Think of *Three Men and a Baby, Casper*, the 1960s TV show *The Courtship of Eddie's Father*, and a multitude of other films and TV shows. (In *Casper*, Mom is literally an angel. But even she comes back from the grave to set Dad straight, admonishing him, among other things, that "French fries are not a breakfast food.")

Unlike the Super Parent plots starring mothers, the theme of single-dad tales is that fathers can't cut it alone. So deeply is anti-father bias ingrained in our collective thinking that in all these stories, Dad isn't just incompetent, he's totally oblivious. It is the child, not Dad, who knows what he or she needs—a mother, of course—and sets out to get it.

How does Junior do that? Most of the time, by finding a good candidate and conspiring to marry her off to poor old blockhead Dad by the final scene. From opening credits to curtain's close, Dad is completely conned by his precocious offspring and never even gets within shouting distance of a clue about what's going on around him.

With these kinds of attitudes so prevalent, it's no wonder divorced dads find themselves way behind in the count before they even come up to bat in the parenting game. They have little or no training in doing it right, so they haven't had the chance to develop experience in day-to-day parenting. Nobody's even tried to teach them how to do it right, so they don't know where to turn for advice. On top of all that, the popular culture is constantly bombarding them with examples of how the parenting efforts of single dads are likely to go completely and spectacularly wrong no matter what they do, so they ought to just leave the whole business up to their kids.

That leaves only one option open to the vast majority of divorced dads, men like you, who are determined to be fully involved and caring parents. You have to be your own teacher.

The Self-made Dad

Art Edelstein was thrust into single parenthood suddenly and quite unwillingly. In the mid-1970s, his marriage came apart when his wife decided she wanted a career and a life of her own. Believing that her husband would be a better parent than she would be, Mrs. Edelstein packed up and moved out, leaving her soon-to-be former husband with their eighteen-month-old son.

Art soon learned firsthand what single mothers go through. He'd work all day and come home exhausted, but there would be chores that had to be done around the house, and he had to take care of his toddler. Art was fortunate enough to earn a good living in advertising, so he was able to hire someone to stay with his son during the day. Even so, his task was made doubly difficult because he knew nothing about being the primary caregiver to a young child, let alone how to run a child-friendly household.

Over the years he sought advice anywhere he could get it, such as "lady friends" who were single parents and took pity on their poor male friend. Mostly, though, Art learned through trial and error. Like the time a girlfriend stayed over-night and had an awkward, unplanned first meeting with Art's little boy in the hallway as they were each making their way to the bathroom. Or the time his son hurt himself falling off the monkey bars in the playground and Art had to rush through the streets of Manhattan to the doctor's office with his sobbing kid in his arms.

If this good man's story sounds familiar to you, that's not surprising. Art's friend, author Avery Corman, was so fas-cinated by his pal's experiences as a postdivorce parent that he fictionalized Art's life in a book, which became a best-seller and then an Oscar-winning motion picture.

It was called *Kramer vs. Kramer.*

The fictional account of Art's life as a divorced dad fairly accurately described his experiences, and he didn't mind the changes made to his story, such as making his son seven or eight years old instead of eighteen months, or having his wayward ex-wife return to seek custody of their son, which didn't happen in real life. He did, however, want Alan Alda to play him on the silver screen, although he admits Dustin Hoffman did okay in the role. And, unlike the movie version and much to his chagrin, Art's sleep-over date the night of the hallway encounter was not JoBeth Williams.

Whether a divorced dad has his kids all the time, half the time or just every other weekend, he faces the same chal-lenges Art Edelstein faced, without the guarantee of a Hol-lywood happy ending. And just like Art, trial and error is usually how a divorced dad learns about the more tedious, mundane aspects of being a day-to-day parent.

Unlike Art Edelstein, however, asking "lady friends" in general and single moms in particular may not be all that appealing an option to you, unless you're fairly thick-skinned. The attitude toward a "househusband" or a single dad frequently takes the form of ridicule, especially from mothers. Women tend to act as if cooking, cleaning, and mak-ing sure the kids' hair is washed three times a week are ar-cane arts a mere male can never master. So they frequently patronize men friends who ask them for a little parenting advice, if they don't demean the poor males' ability to parent outright. I don't know about you, but there's nothing more annoying to me than a woman shaking her head and rolling her eyes about the way I raise my kid.

Too often, a divorced dad will be out somewhere with his child during the middle of the day and will find himself the only male in a sea of moms at a department store, all of whom seem to be staring at him as if he were an object of pity or an ax murderer (depending on whether he is in control of his kid at the time or trying desperately to rein the kid in). I once stalked out of a McDonald's with Alex in tow after being handed a free brochure on parenting that constantly referred to the parent as "she." And everyone, males and females, are routinely forced to endure long lectures from their mothers or sisters or other female relatives about the "right" and "wrong" way to raise a kid.

If you have a female friend who's a single mother and is willing to help you without belittling what you're going through, by all means accept the help. But you're better off becoming a self-made student of parenting. You don't need the ability to give birth to understand commonsense needs like child locks for your cabinets and plastic bumpers for the sharp edges of your coffee table. You just have to reorient yourself to think about such things, and be open to picking up tips wherever you can.

Some of the best sources for such advice are the national parenting magazines, which are monthly gold mines of useful information on how to raise kids. But remember, they're geared toward women readers. So grit your teeth and plow through all the "I am woman, hear me roar" rhetoric. It'll be worth your while.

Don't expect to find a lot of data specific to fathers in these publications. At best, you'll find only a column or two on the subject of male parenting in every issue, usually geared to and written by married men. These columns mostly contain feel-good anecdotes about the joys of nuclear fathering and rarely offer specific advice for unmarried dads. Nonetheless, in terms of general parenting, they can be welcome sources of good, solid suggestions to an information-starved divorced dad.

Parenting magazine has a fairly elaborate home page on America Online, and I hit it regularly. There you can find not only stories the publication has run but also information on a long laundry list of topics, from how to handle children at different ages, to where to take them on outings, how to clothe them, what to say to them, and a myriad of other subjects.

If you're a savvy student of parenting, you can find good advice in a number of unlikely places. One resource, in fact, may be in front of you every time you dash into a convenience store for a bottle of soda or take your clothes to the dry cleaner, even if you've never noticed it. It's the local parenting publication, and almost every town or city neighborhood has one—many of them free. They're usually distributed through various retail outlets like bookstores, clothing shops, and supermarkets, and sometimes through the library. Articles in these magazines and tabloids are written by local experts and can be extremely useful. Also, the lifestyle sections of many daily newspapers regularly run parenting tips and features that can provide a bonanza of actionable info for divorced dads.

When your little girl runs up to you on one of your Saturdays and begs you to save the baby bird that fell out of its nest in the tree next to your place, do you know what to do? Are you aware that sunglasses are as important as sunscreen in protecting your child against the sun? You are? Great. How do you choose the right pair? When it's time to go back to school, what's the most important purchase you can make for your kid? All these subjects and many more were covered in my local newspaper or in one of the three giveaway parenting magazines distributed in my neighborhood in the last year. I'm fortunate enough to live within the distribution area of what I believe is the best local parenting magazine in

America, *L.A. Parent*, but there are undoubtedly similarly helpful publications readily available where you live.

By the way, if you have an idea where a downed baby bird's nest is, it's okay to return the bird to its nest. If you can't find the bird's home, and it's in danger on the ground, put it in a box or an open bird cage and leave it close to where you found it. Every baby bird has a distinct cry, and its parents will eventually come for it. (But if you find a rabbit nest unattended in the daytime, leave it alone. Bunnies feed at night and Mom is probably out rustling up some dinner— literally.)

As for sunglasses, you don't judge them by the darkness of the lens, but by whether they absorb 99 percent of UV radiation. Polarized lenses aren't enough; the label must specify that the shades are UV ray absorbent. It's wise to choose unbreakable plastic for lenses and frames.

Orthopedic doctors advise parents equipping their kids for school to make safe backpacks a top priority item. You want to look for special kid-size backpacks, padded backs and straps, curved straps, even waist belts if they're available. The experts add that if your child cannot pick up a loaded pack easily in one hand, it probably weighs too much. No matter what the weight, the load should be evenly distributed. And be alert to your young one complaining about shoulder and neck pain.

The astute student of parenting also will make periodic forays to his library and local bookstore to stock up on parenting books. Again, almost none of these books, if any, will focus exclusively on divorced-dad parenting. Still, some will contain a chapter or two on the subject, and a healthy chunk of their general counsel is directly applicable to your situation. On a broad level, the information you find in these books tends to be repetitive; there are universals that every divorced parent must confront and there are only so many ways to describe them. And what specific information does exist for divorced dads is usually written by a woman and the language may not be tailored to men. Nevertheless, every book will include at least one and usually several little gems of specific advice you can use in your own life, and it's well worth digging for them.

Off the literary self-help avenues, don't expect your still-hitched pals to be any help whatsoever. Mark Ludwick, the award-winning divorced dad we met earlier, tried talking to married male friends about how they handled various day-to-day details like ongoing discipline, setting household policies on such things as TV watching, and so on, but none of them did any of that in their households. Predictably, the married dads always left those parenting details to their wives. My two best friends, both married fathers, were more interested in the vicarious thrills they received from accounts of my suddenly single lifestyle than in providing me with any useful parenting help, let alone support.

Churches, synagogues, and mosques can be comforting and educational places for a divorced dad to turn. Most of them have parenting programs of some kind—the parenting course that launched Mark Ludwick on his award-winning divorced-dad journey was a church-sponsored program—and of course, the leaders of such institutions usually include the gift of wise counsel among their many contributions to the community.

Not so the theological fathering groups. The fundamentalist Promise Keepers and the Nation of Islam, which produced the Million Man March on Washington, are the best known, but there seems to be a new one every day. They do a lot of clapping and cheering and making grand speeches in football stadiums about the importance of fathers in family life, and we've seen how good they are at organizing marches. To the degree they keep divorced dads and unmarried fathers from becoming absent parents, these groups serve a worthwhile purpose. However, most of these organizations appear designed to keep men married, not to help them be good fathers. And just as the politicians who spit and spout about family values have their own agenda, these groups appear to be geared primarily to convert you to their religious or ethnocentric point of view, and only secondarily to help you parent. (They get indignant when you mention that, of course.)

According to the Census Bureau, the number of families of any kind in which Dad stays at home zoomed from 700,000 in 1980 to 1.6 million in 1993. Among households with working parents, those headed by single fathers are increasing faster than any other kind. And in a 1995 study, a research group found that 10 percent of American husbands were "designated homemakers," up from just 2 percent in 1986.

Their Home Away from Home

Many successful divorced dads begin their postdivorce parenting before they've even moved out. They choose where they live after the divorce by how child-friendly the environment is, looking for things like nearby parks and other single-parent families in the neighborhood, apartment building, or condo complex. When possible, some dads even take their kids with them to scout out a possible apartment or neighborhood. Involving your kids in the logistics of your postdivorce life is in general, a good idea. It gives them a sense of ownership, reduces their fear of instability, and provides you and them with additional opportunities to create your own history independent of their life with their mother.

Inside your place, the principle is the same: involve your child as much as possible in making this new house a home and give the child a sense of ownership. In some family courts, judges now insist that noncustodial parents provide a separate bedroom with a separate door and a good bed for their children. If you are unable to provide these things when your kid stays over, you should come as close to that arrangement as possible. *Kids need their own, identifiable space.* If a separate room is out of the question, at least start by getting a sofa bed or cot specifically for the child.

You don't need to nor should you recreate a theme park in your apartment, but you should strive to create what one divorced dad calls a "child-centered household." When you do get your daughter her own room, for example, help her put up posters or paint one wall of her room.

In addition, personal items specific to your place can add domestic texture and reassure your children. They should have separate toys that stay at your house all the time. Your kids will always drag a few things back and forth, of course, but it's a good idea to have even just a few playthings they identify with you. Likewise, keep two or three changes of clothes at your place, a separate toothbrush, hair dryer, coloring books and, yes, perhaps even a "Dad's house" backpack and other regularly used items.

At my house, Alex has his own bright blue laundry hamper in his bedroom, his own soap and bubble bath in the bathroom, his own videotape and audio cassette drawer in the living room, and even his own set of pencils for doing his homework during overnight stays. None of these things cost a lot of money, and they contribute greatly to giving Alex a sense that my place is his place as well.

Just a little duplication of everyday items will create a homelike setting for your child, and it has a practical purpose in that your kid won't always have to carry a suitcase back and forth. Besides, inevitably there will be times when Mom forgets to pack socks or a change of underwear, and if you have your own clothes stash, that's one less extra trip you have to make.

Not only do these things give children, even adolescents, a sense of permanence and security when they're with you, they also have the added benefit of reducing the need to communicate with your ex-wife. If you don't have to endure the aggravation of going back to her house to get a missing item of clothing, you might avoid the urge to comment on proper visitation preparation. Plus she's probably going to criticize what you buy your child anyway, so you might as well minimize her chances to do so by having "Dad toys" that don't travel back and forth between your home and hers.

That trick can work both ways, too. Debbie Nigro, author, single mom, speaker, and star of the syndicated national radio show *Working Mom on the Run*, suggests that if your kid brings to your house a new toy you consider inappropriate from his mother, her boyfriend or husband, or her relatives, don't make an issue out of it. Just say, "Please play with that toy only at Mommy's house."

A Sense of Belonging

So far, we've talked about how to create the kind of environment your child can be comfortable living in, but what you do during the times your kid shares that environment with you is equally important. It takes more than a separate room or a second toothbrush to make a divorced dad's house his children's home. You can make them feel comfortable in a thousand and one little ways, each of which is another brick in the foundation of your relationship with them.

This is one of the few areas of divorced parenting in which there is a refreshing unanimity of opinion among the experts. Everyone counsels that you should strive to make the time your child spends with you as unspectacular as possible. This doesn't mean swearing off dad-only trips to Walt Disney World or the mountains in the summer. Those are special times, just as they would be if you were all still part of a nuclear family. But nothing reassures a child faster than the mundane stuff of living. When your children are with you, have fun and live each moment to the fullest, but also make those moments integral parts of the rhythm of your kids' lives.

Take your child with you when you do simple, ordinary, everyday things, like going to the bank or getting the oil in your car changed. The more mundane, the better. I make a point, for example, of having Alex with me when I get the car washed. He throws coins into the wishing well by the waiting area. It's become a tradition in our divorced-dad home.

Many dads refuse to leave their kid with a baby-sitter during the times when they have custody. Every moment with their children is just too precious. I understand. In five years, I've never left Alex with a baby-sitter. You can always rearrange a date; you never get back lost moments with your child. But one thing you absolutely should do, assuming you live nearby, is to arrange play dates for your kids' friends to come over to your house or for your kid to go to their houses during your weekends.

Again, arranging play dates reinforces the normalcy you are trying to restore to their lives, and it also reaffirms your parental role. Besides, it's just plain fun for your kids. I love it when one of my son's friends comes over for the first time, and Alex proudly marches the kid around my apartment, giving him the Cook's tour of Dad's place. He's proud of his father, he's taken ownership of his dad's place—and Dad feels, if only briefly, that maybe he will be able to get the hang of this parenting thing after all.

Little moments like washing the car with Dad or having your buddies over for a play date are the ones we remember the most vividly. For you, a divorced dad, every one of these "life snapshots" helps to *create a mutual history* with your children, something unique to you and them that cannot be taken away. These moments are protection against a divorced father's greatest fear: that their mother will turn the children against him. The necessity of accumulating these little life moments with your children is the reason that, despite the vocal opposition of some psychologists, feminists, and custodial moms, your visitation arrangement should include at least occasional school night sleep-over privileges. This is especially important if you have teenagers, who inevitably will get caught in an emotional tug of war between their desire to see their dad and their plans to be with their friends on the weekends.

Again, you may not be able to do some of these things exactly the way the experts suggest you do them, just as you may not have the resources to provide a separate room for your kid. But, to rewrite an old axiom, "Necessity is the father of creativity"; you'll think of acceptable alternatives. Besides, many of the opportunities you and your children will have for small, shared experiences have nothing to do with economic circumstance. Anybody can turn on a hose, fill a bucket with water, and wash the car with the kids.

Here are some of the ways two divorced dads built unbreakable bonds with their kids.

Every year when school lets out, ten-year-old Laura boards a plane on the West Coast where she lives with her mom and flies a few hours east to spend the summer with her dad. He picks her up and takes her . . . home. At her dad's place, Laura leaves her bags in her own room and runs outside to play with her friends next door. Even though Laura lives there only a few weeks out of the year, she's part of the neighborhood, enthusiastically joining her dad and their neighbors for backyard barbecues and watching fireworks on the Fourth of July.

Laura often accompanies her dad to his office. He owns a small business with about ten employees, all of whom look forward to having Laura around. She even has her own place in her dad's office where she can draw and play on the computer.

Mark Ludwick also brought his daughter Stephanie to work when he ran his own business. She had her own desk there, with a little phone (not a real one, of course), and she would help the secretaries put mailings together. For a while, Stephanie actually thought she was part of the secretarial pool, but the great thing was, she felt important to her dad. She was a part of his life.

The Value of a Dollar

Verities become verities for a reason. Clichés don't arise by accident. Most of the hoary old sayings we grow up with contain at least a grain of truth, or they'd never have survived to become hoary. The simple beliefs and basic way of life of a more innocent, more rural America still resonate with the force of truth.

How do you teach kids the value of the dollar? By giving them an allowance. How do kids earn an allowance? By doing their chores.

If possible, the tasks you assign your children at your place should at least approximate the chores they're assigned in their mom's home. Some of this is basic "clean up your mess" stuff and is only indirectly related to an allowance. That includes activities such as clearing off the table after eating and bringing the dishes to the sink (usually washing them as well); making their beds; cleaning their rooms. The last thing Alex does before I take him home on Sunday evening is make a sweep of the apartment to see that he's put all of his toys away.

There also should be some chores unique to you and your kids' mutual history—taking out the dog, if you have one; watering your plants—little things that require small effort but pay big dividends in the learning-responsibility department.

Assign one or two regular chores for your child to do to earn an allowance. Doing homework promptly and without complaining may even be one of them, although I tend to think of that as one of the basic responsibilities kids have to learn to do for its own sake. The allowance should be small, no more than $10 to $20 per week for preadolescents and teenagers, less if they're younger. But the sooner they begin to understand the idea that money isn't accumulated by magic but by effort, the better off you'll be.

These tips may sound embarrassingly old-fashioned, but,

boy, do they work as instructional tools. Your children learn to equate honest work with honest reward, but more importantly, they interact with you in a classic parent-as-teacher way that is vital to their upbringing.

We no longer live in a country where most of us will have our kids feeding the chickens or plowing the fields to earn their allowances, but the principles for having kids do chores are as durable and as valuable as they ever were. It is particularly important for a divorced dad to institute such policies at his home, because chores and allowances are comforting reminders to your kids that although you no longer live with them, you are still their dad.

Kiss the Chef

My mom was a gourmet cook, and she could make dishes so delicious that your mouth would water for weeks. Still, some of my most cherished childhood memories are of warm summer evenings when my father would take over the kitchen.

He always made the same meal, a simple, hearty, inexpensive factory worker's dinner that kept him alive during his years as an impoverished college student in France before the Second World War: broiled steak smothered in margarine and marinated in minced onions that were cooked to a tongue-tingling crispness; thin, delicate French fries; iceberg lettuce salad with an oil and vinegar dressing; fresh fruit and cheese for dessert. What made this dinner so wonderful, though, wasn't its taste, the infrequency of its serving, or even its evocative European origin. What made it so special was the fact that my dad cooked it.

Perhaps I shouldn't have been surprised, then, when I discovered that the technique divorced dads used most frequently to cement their postdivorce relationship with their children was cooking. When asked to give examples of activities they did with and for their kids that had a big effect on their relationship, every one of the fathers interviewed for this book included cooking on his list.

Usually there's a specific dish that defines dining tradition at Dad's place. One divorced father makes pizza from scratch with his two daughters. They knead the dough, he adds the flour and water and cuts up the pie. Presto! A special Dad-and-daughters evening without spending a lot of money. At the Krauss home in Manhattan, Michael's two girls invite their friends to stay the night with the promise of one of Dad's big pancake breakfast sleep-over specials the next morning.

"I'm picking up recipes now and really getting into it," sums up a divorced dad in California. His specialties? "Guy stuff like barbecued ribs."

Indeed, the best thing about cooking traditions at divorced-dad homes is that they are very masculine variations on a traditional female area of expertise. Guys don't pretend to be fancy chefs and make their kids eggs Benedict, duck à l'Orange, or seaweed salad. But they don't mimic mom's everyday dinners either. Few of the special meals dads whip up for their kids are of the conventional macaroni-and-cheese or hot dog variety. These fathers serve simple, inexpensive foods that are easy to prepare, but they add a touch of creative magic to them. How can homemade pizza, pancake breakfast specials, and barbecued ribs not be forever embedded in kids' minds as Dad's special treat to them?

So if you do only one thing to build a special tradition between you and your kids, make it cooking. Because when it comes to good divorced-dad parenting, *a man's place is in the kitchen.*

Taming the Tube

Is television a parent's friend or a relentless foe? As long we've had TV, we've wrestled with that question, and there really isn't a clear-cut answer. One thing is certain, though:

television is a dominant influence in your kid's life. Your household TV policy, therefore, is critical to your day-to-day parenting. Most dads go to an extreme: either they treat the set as a pulsating electronic poison and try to keep the kids away from it entirely, or they use the tube as a kind of electronic baby-sitter. Neither is effective.

Bob Keeshan, adored by millions of kids and parents alike as Captain Kangaroo, offers the following counsel:

"I hate it when a parent tells me, 'We don't have TV, we put it in a closet two years ago.' Well, that's dumb. What you're telling me when you say that is that you can't control the TV. There are good programs, fun programs, that kids can use to grow on. You have the ability to turn it on when it's appropriate and turn it off when it isn't. Of course, that same parent usually goes on to tell you what happened on *NYPD Blue* last week."

What Keeshan means is, if you're proactive rather than victimized by the thing, it's quite possible to construct a viable household television policy. You can make your TV set a tool instead of an obstacle in your divorced-dad efforts. Doing this can also help reduce tension between you and your ex-wife, because custodial mothers love to grouse about how much TV their miserable ex-husbands let their kids watch.

Here are three solid tips for forming workable household TV rules, based on the advice of experts such as Keeshan and others:

1. *Control your TV.* You can't eliminate the boob tube from your kids' lives and you certainly can't eliminate their desire for it. So go with the flow: discuss a variety of programs you don't mind your children watching, on both educational and regular channels, and pick a few. The choices shouldn't all be yours; let your kids pick one or two shows. If you can afford them and your cable company carries them, subscribe to the Disney Channel, Nickelodeon, or the Cartoon Network.

2. *Make TV time an opportunity for a life snapshot.* Watch together, make popcorn and put it in a big bowl between you, hold hands if you have a little one. When something happens or somebody says something in a show you're watching together that makes you wince (plenty of opportunities for that, as we all know), discuss it with your kids. Be honest about things you don't like and explain why you don't like them. And get your children to ponder the implications of what they're watching with open-ended questions like "What would you do if that were you, and why?" or "What other ways can you think of to handle that situation?"

3. *Don't turn the set on all the time.* The Academy of Pediatrics recommends that children should watch no more than two hours a day. You probably should keep the small screen dark, in fact, until the evening. In the morning, you should be getting your kids ready for school if it's a weeknight stay-over, returning them to their mother if it's a weekend, making sure you and your kids eat breakfast; or, if it's a weekday, dropping them off at school with enough margin left over to get to work on time. In the afternoon, your children should be out playing with friends or doing homework.

Besides, afternoons are when you want to watch baseball.

CHAPTER 7

◆

Season With Care:
Handling the Holidays

Tradition is a guide, not a jailer.

—W. SOMERSET MAUGHAM

One recent Christmas season, a family therapist faced a ticklish situation she was at a complete loss to resolve. The therapist was having a difficult time helping a daughter of divorcing parents cope during the holidays. She had tried referring the couple to support groups for guidance; she had attempted to reassure the girl that she was still loved and that things would settle down; she tried everything she or any other counselor she spoke to could think of. Nothing worked. The child was inconsolable.

The reason nothing worked, the terrible thing that made this poor little girl so distraught, was the season. She was afraid Santa Claus would be mad at her family for breaking up.

A holiday is an emotional minefield for everybody, a boiling pot full of dashed hopes and comparisons of what is with what might have been. Because of their specialness, holidays practically force us to take stock of our lives, bringing back to the surface the feelings of anger, guilt, sadness, and remorse we are able to suppress during the rest of the year.

The media, of course, don't help, alternately bombarding us with two different images, each equally painful. We either see impossibly well-adjusted nuclear families beaming and showering one another with unconditional love, or we're subjected to a parade of dysfunctional, miserable folks forced to interact with people they don't like just because they're related to each other.

Holiday movies also swing wildly between these two extremes—either *It's a Wonderful Life* or we're *Scrooged*. Holidays perform a neurotic tap dance on the brains of divorced parents, who must carry on despite being bombarded with reminders of the kind of Norman Rockwell family life they "should" have or tormented with images of the kind of miserable loners they might become.

For most divorced parents, holidays are both unbearably poignant and unbelievably weird. Compounding the stress is the unavoidable fact that at holiday time, you're compelled to interact with your ex and her family. And you have to deal with the unfortunate ability of these celebrations to catalyze unrealistic hopes in your kids about getting their parents back together, if only for an evening.

If your child was quite young when you divorced, you may escape some of the pressures. Or, as one divorced dad so aptly put it, "Billy was young enough when we divorced that a dual family is all he knows. He didn't have eight or nine years of Christmases to forget."

But whether or not they remember Christmases past, during the holidays, your children will be as torn between the two of you as they always are. Because it's the holiday season, though, the intensity is ratcheted up a notch. Plus, with all the gift-giving, partying, merry-making, fireworks-watching, barbecue-having, big-meal eating, major motion picture-opening traditions that mark any holiday, there are also that many more opportunities for the kids to indulge their appetites for manipulating Mom and Dad.

Naturally, both you and your ex-wife want to spend the holidays with the kids, so a lot of additional negotiation and planning is necessary for both of you to be satisfied. This creates a nightmare of logistical maneuvering that even the most detailed divorce settlement can't begin to address.

Will confuses dozens of people every year by trying to explain his holiday travel schedule. When you have six kids of your own, three who live with you and three who live with their mom, two stepkids from your second marriage, and biological parents living as much as six hundred miles away, you need the logistical genius of a Patton to keep everybody satisfied.

Here's how one year went: Will celebrated Christmas early with his three oldest kids on December 22, at home in Detroit. The next day, he drove to Pittsburgh with the kids and stayed the night. Their biological mother, who lives in Delaware, came up to Pittsburgh (halfway between Dad's house and Mom's house), picked up the three kids and returned to Delaware on the 23rd. Will drove back to Detroit, where he spent Christmas Day with his wife and her two kids. The next day, she drove to Cincinnati with her two kids and dropped them off with their biological dad, then turned around and drove right back to Detroit.

On the 27th, Will drove back to Pittsburgh and left his car at the airport there. He then flew to Philadelphia (the closest airport to Delaware), and stayed in Delaware for the next couple of days to see his youngest three kids, who live with their mom.

Meanwhile, Will's current wife drove back to Cincinnati to see old friends and pick up her kids, returning on the 30th of December. That same day, Will's ex-wife drove his oldest three kids to Pittsburgh, where everybody stayed the night. The next morning, a Sunday, Will drove from Delaware to the Philadelphia airport, picked up his car at nine A.M., drove to Pittsburgh, picked up his three oldest kids (the ones who live with him) and drove back home to Michigan.

The next day was New Year's. Will slept in.

Sort of takes your breath away, doesn't it? But you too can handle the holidays, travel schedules and all. Here, as always, keeping interparent conflict out of the festivities will help mightily. Equitable child-sharing is not only possible, it is eminently doable. You might even be able to enjoy the holidays, if you follow some basic guidelines—ten, to be exact.

The Divorced Dad's Holiday Top Ten

Rule #1: Don't believe everything you read. By all means, consult the experts when trying to devise a workable holiday policy, but be aware that you're going to have to modify some or all of the tips you pick up from divorce help books. When they stick to generalities, the experts' advice is sound and gender-neutral, but they can be way off base when writing specifically about noncustodial fathers and holidays. They also have a tendency to depend on touchy-feely suggestions that don't work very well or just plain sound silly to men, like joining a support group anytime anything happens to you that's even the slightest bit uncomfortable, or making up cute little 12-step–type names for things.

For instance, several experts warn divorced dads that they might have a tough time with Father's Day, because the June holiday conjures up images of the family they've lost, especially when they don't get to see their kids. On the contrary, most divorced dads I know love Father's Day because it reaffirms their importance in their children's lives. The holiday is also popular with fathers because, assuming they live nearby and their ex-wife is halfway sane, divorced dads always have their kids on Father's Day. Even many fathers who live far away often get to spend that particular holiday with their kids because it occurs in the summer, when most noncustodial and distanced fathers have custody of their children anyway.

The dads who don't love Father's Day aren't saddened by it, they're contemptuous of it. "It's a Hallmark holiday," sniffs one, who adds that "on Mother's Day, the pastor in our church would lecture all the fathers in the congregation about how we should love and respect our children's mothers. But on Father's Day, all we heard from him were tirades about what lousy fathers we all were."

Rule #2: Negotiate holiday arrangements with your ex-wife months in advance. Many divorce agreements will include detailed provisions for when Dad gets custody of the kids, usually alternating years for the big celebrations like Christmas and Thanksgiving, on his birthday and on Father's Day. Mom gets similar privileges: her birthday and Mother's Day. Easter is usually included in the settlement as well. But that leaves plenty of other holidays and vacation periods to negotiate. After the two of you decide on who will get whom and when, you must give your ex precise details well in advance, and she should return the favor, or the holidays will quickly become a series of unpleasant battles between the two of you. This is especially true if either of you wants to take the kids out of town for the holidays. And once made, don't break plans unless you absolutely have to; it's not only rude, it's a provocation. And your children may not understand why you're not doing what you said you'd do.

I made that mistake while writing this book—I had agreed to have Alex stay with me for the two-week winter vacation, because his grandparents, who lived nearby, were going out of town and I didn't want to spend the money to put Alex in daycare for the fortnight. But less than a week into his vacation and almost halfway into the schedule we had agreed upon before winter break began, I realized that I needed a day or two off to finish writing. And I took it.

My ex-wife was left with no alternative but to take two

sudden days off she could ill afford. That rash decision (I really didn't need two whole days to complete my task) was the most unfair thing I've done in our postdivorce relationship, and it didn't feel good when I realized how wrong I had been. More to the point, my relationship with my ex-wife was strained for a week or two during an already stress-filled time. I paid dearly for those two days.

You also must be fair about sharing your children during holiday periods. Your kids don't just have the right to two parents, they also have the right to four grandparents, any number of aunts and uncles, and cousins to hang out with on the holidays. That means each side of the child's family should be given the opportunity to see the child every other holiday at a minimum, and at the very least they should have the right to phone your kid during holiday periods when you don't have the child.

One solution that works pretty well for many divorced dads and their ex-wives is to split the big holidays rather than alternate them. For example, the kids spend Christmas Eve at her house and Christmas Day at your place, or they celebrate the first night of Passover with your family and the second night with hers.

Divorced parents with more than one child will sometimes split them up at holiday time; one child spends the holiday with her and one with you, and so on. This is a bad idea. The kids can get jealous of one another, and somebody is always missing out on being with somebody under these arrangements.

Rule #3: Make your own traditions. Just like your day-to-day life with your children, the holidays you spend together should be uniquely yours as well. You make that happen the same way you build a mutual history, by starting your own traditions, things that you and your kids do together every year, either the same kinds of things you did on the holidays when you were an intact nuclear family or entirely different traditions. This is considerably easier, of course, if your children were very young when you divorced, because there isn't much of a history of family celebrations. But even the venerable traditions you all counted on when you were together can be modified to fit your new divorced-dad life.

Every Christmas morning, Will's great aunt would cook a special treat for the whole family: aebelskivers, mouthwatering Swedish pancakes, sometimes filled with delicious sweet stuff. Aebelskiver-making is a big deal, including a special cast-iron aebelskiver skillet, a secret recipe, and much anticipation.

After Will's great aunt died, he became the keeper of the aebelskiver tradition. Come Christmas morning, he would be in the kitchen playing aebelskiver chef for his household. When he was divorced, however, the tradition became difficult to maintain, since Will's ex-wife and three of his kids live hundreds of miles away. So every Christmas season, Will packs up a skillet, a blender, and his secret recipe and flies out to see his kids. He checks into a suite at the hotel, fills the refrigerator with all the necessary ingredients, and invites the tribe over to the suite for an aebelskiver feast. Thus the aebelskiver tradition lives on, albeit a few days late. And nobody ever leaves Dad's hotel room hungry at Christmastime.

Another great way to build your own holiday traditions is for you and your little guys or gals to travel every year. The travel industry has lately discovered that single parents do actually vacation with their kids from time and time, and special programs or deals abound. According to the U.S. Travel Data Center, in fact, single-parent families took 8 percent of all trips of one hundred miles or more in 1991. That percentage was up from 6 percent in 1985. Club Med, several cruise lines, and travel companies specializing in single-parent traveling all cater to the unmarried with children. With a little preparation, annual trips can be a great way to bond with your kid.

Alex is with me every Christmas week (Christmas Day is my birthday, anyway), so one year, the two of us drove to

Sacramento and celebrated the holiday with my best friend Bill and his family, who annually transform their house into Christmas World.

The kitchen table groans with seasonal food, holiday music plays all day and all night, the house is decorated from top to bottom in red and green, and the living room is dominated by a monster tree with enough lights on it to illuminate a small municipality. (If you've ever been to Sacramento during the holidays, you'll know that Bill's house is typical of the Christmas frenzy that sweeps through the city every winter. Sacramento folks celebrate Christmas with such indefatigable gusto, you'd think the town was in the North Pole instead of northern California.)

When the weather warms, Alex and I spend a weekend together at Disneyland during spring break or Memorial Day weekend, whichever falls on one of my regularly scheduled weekends with him. Alex and I look forward eagerly to these annual father and son traditions. And my ex-wife can count on at least one holiday week and one additional noncourt ordered weekend off every year, so she usually plans a trip somewhere as well.

Being a divorced dad and child on vacation can be expensive, however. Some single-parent premiums can be as much as 60 percent above normal rates. You or your travel agent will have to shop around. And ask some questions before you book, such as the availability of supervised children's activities, daycare, and baby-sitting. If you have a preadolescent or teenager, another important query you might not think of until too late is: does your room have a separate dressing area to offer some privacy?

Rule #4: Do not share the holidays. One of my divorced-dad friends has a very strange relationship with his ex-wife. They were best friends before they got married, so when they broke up, they just returned to their premarried relationship. He hangs out with her and her boyfriend all the time, she likes his girlfriend, his girlfriend likes her, the kids like everybody. One big, happy, nonnuclear family. Naturally, they all celebrate the holidays together too.

The experts hedge their bets on this subject. On one hand, there are those who won't advise you not to do it, exactly, but they'll damn the practice with faint praise, using guarded phrases like "if you feel you have a healthy enough relationship with your former spouse . . ." On the other hand, the shared-family contingent thinks holidaying together is bloody marvelous. They claim that giving kids a healthy extended family full of step this-and-that and current and former in-laws, is a good thing. Supporters of shared holidays also minimize the critics' claim that celebrating with your former spouse and your kids just encourages the youngsters to harbor false hopes of getting their parents back together, since children will hold on to those unrealistic expectations all their lives no matter what.

The dad we just described is quite unusual. No matter how healthy the extended family is, there's bound to be barely disguised discontent, frustration, or envy brewing underneath the bonhomie, because it's natural and unavoidable that everybody's going to be hypersensitive at holiday time.

The first three years after my divorce, I was invited to my ex-mother-in-law's house for Thanksgiving dinner. Alex would ask his grandmother and mother to invite me. But I decided not to go the fourth year, although I was very careful to explain to my son why I wouldn't share the evening with him and Mom and grandparents anymore. I told him that it was uncomfortable for the adults to get together like this as if we were all still an intact family, and we didn't think it was fair to him to pretend that we were still nuclear.

Spending holidays together as if you were still married really is an invitation to trouble, a nasty and unnecessary fight waiting to happen. You'd be better off politely declining and telephoning during the evening to wish everybody a happy holiday.

There is one exception to this rule: your child's birthday. The noncustodial parent should at least make an extended appearance on the child's birthday. Children, especially younger ones, regard birthday party participation as a test of parental love. If you can, co-produce the birthday party with your ex-wife and split the cost. Do this no matter who has visitation on the birthday or the day of the party. Another good idea: hold the party on neutral ground, like Discovery Zone or Chuck E. Cheese or the local pizzeria.

If you do co-produce the party, minimize the chances of sparking an argument by being very detailed about which parent is responsible for what, down to the napkins, paper plates, and balloons. At the party itself, be prepared to be with your ex and probably her family as well for a few hours at least, and use the anger-handling techniques we discussed in chapters Three and Five to get you through it.

Your child will thank you.

Rule #5: Do not make surprise visits. You might be inclined to show up at her house on Christmas Eve, bearing gifts. Or appear at her door at Eastertime. Maybe stop by unannounced the first day of Hanukkah. This is a bad idea at any time, but particularly during holiday celebration. It is even more of an invitation to trouble than sharing the holiday with your ex-wife, because now you really are attempting to cut into her time with the kids. If you miss them during the holidays they're with their mom, give them a call. Do not surprise them. Do not talk your way into an invitation to come over, either. The resentment you will create will be just as strong.

Rule #6: Consider what the children want. Some psychologists believe that children have the right to be consulted about everything that affects them, and that the fairest holiday solution for divorced parents is for the children to go where they want to go during the holidays. I don't know any parent who agrees with that lamebrained idea, but on the off chance you are one of them, let me tell you right now this also is not a smart move. Children neither need nor really want that responsibility, and anyway, what kids want more than anything is to be with both parents in one home, which of course is not possible. That being said, however, in some scenarios consulting the children of divorce about your plans for the holidays is okay.

If your kids are very young, it certainly won't hurt to take into account what kind of celebration they like best. Is your son the gregarious sort who loves large, hearty gatherings? Is your daughter more happy with small celebrations with just you or a few other people close to her? After you pass through the two-year divorce gauntlet, arranging holiday events with your kids' preferences in mind may become almost reflexive. By then, your new life together will feel more real, the kids are likely settled into the postdivorce routine, and they'll let you know in word, deed and attitude how they feel about the new holiday customs you and their mother are creating.

In any circumstance, teenagers ought to be asked what they'd like to do for the holidays, and probably will have some good ideas about how to arrange the time fairly for all concerned.

The final decision on holiday plans, of course, should always rest with you and your ex-wife.

Rule #7: Two of everything isn't bad. When you're a Christmas baby like I am, people always think you get short-changed at the holidays, so they buy you twice as many presents as they buy for everybody else. I didn't grow up terminally spoiled because I was lucky enough to get duplicate gifts every year, and neither will your kid. But it's still a good idea to work with your ex on gift-giving. Perhaps you join forces to buy a bike, or jointly agree that Junior already has enough action figures to launch a global conflict, and not getting one more won't ruin his enjoyment of Hanukkah; or that your princess is too young to get lipstick even though she's begging for some in her stocking. In the main, though, give your kids whatever you want to. They really won't be damaged for life. Trust me.

Rule #8: Don't be "Maudlin Man." Celebrate the holidays when you don't have your kids, too. Go out with friends, go to a party, enjoy! Your children won't forget you because they didn't spend one Easter with you. Take a tip from your ex here: custodial moms often take advantage of a few days of freedom with a little R&R at a resort. My ex often relaxes in Cabo San Lucas during the winter festivities, for example.

Childless holidays are a perfect opportunity for you to reward yourself with that just-for-me trip you've wanted to take but couldn't find the time to plan. One divorced dad goes into the mountains or unwinds at a spa every holiday he's not with his kid. Another makes sure his chalet is booked for a ski getaway during the holidays his daughter stays with her mom. I go to Las Vegas if I'm feeling like a bad boy, or up to the majestic forests of Big Sur if I'm feeling spiritual.

These little adventures during holidays when the kids are with their mother can work wonders for a divorced dad's peace of mind. Getting morose and feeling sorry for yourself is senseless, not to mention undignified. And your children will feel less guilty if they know you had fun just like they did.

Rule #9: Celebrate with other single parents if you can. In the course of building a life as a divorced dad, you will naturally seek out other single parents, preferably of the attractive, charming, female kind. Seek them out on the holidays as well. You'd be surprised how good that will make everybody feel.

Rule #10: Gifts are not acceptable reasons to pick a fight. A radio commercial running in Los Angeles for a local bank and promoting holiday season loans features the voice of a harried shopper frantically ticking off all of the gifts he has to remember to buy before Christmas. All but one of the about-to-be-purchased presents on his long list are pretty nice, except for the "fruitcake for my ex-wife."

The commercial may be tongue-in-cheek, but the idea behind it is serious stuff indeed. Gifts are symbolic expressions of how you feel about a person and, more important, your image of who that person is. As such, they are loaded emotional weapons for any divorced dad. But gifts for your ex-wife, ironically, can also help cement your bond with your child and offer you an opportunity to do what you do best—be a teacher.

Let's start with the first point, gifts as symbolic expressions. This is for those fortunate dads with a positive enough relationship with their ex that they exchange gifts at holiday time. I can hear the jaws of those of you whose relationships with your exes are less than pleasant drop with a thud, but a lot of divorced couples still do exchange gifts at holiday time.

My recommendation is: if you can avoid it, do so. She's your child's mother but she's no longer related to you in any way. If she gives you a gift, okay, you have to return the compliment. Also your kids may force the issue. I know of many instances of muttering parents being led into a mall by their young ones because the children demand, "Daddy, buy Mommy something" for Christmas. But buy something neutral. Gift certificates to department stores or bookstores are great ways to be considerate without making a statement that might be misinterpreted.

When it comes to your kids, however, you should participate in their gift selection process with gusto. Help them pick out a gift for Mommy on Christmas or Hanukkah and, on Mother's Day, you may want to help them choose and send her flowers. Then wrap the present with them. (Don't help them deliver the gift, of course.)

Boy, do kids respond to this. Their faces light up like the Christmas tree at Rockefeller Center. The reason is, you're teaching them how to show consideration. You're not just avoiding conflict, you are actively helping to build a peace between your ex-wife and yourself by helping the children make their mother happy. I've seen kids absolutely beam when their dads do this for them. It may feed the reconcili-ation fantasy a bit, but it's worth it to see your kids so happy. So do it, and damn the experts.

I've given you some ideas on making a home, giving gifts, handling emotions, and staying involved. Now let's get down to the nitty gritty: getting back into the social whirl. If you've got more than visions of sugar plums dancing in your head, read on for some ideas on how to ease yourself back into postdivorce dating.

CHAPTER 8

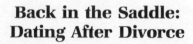

Back in the Saddle:
Dating After Divorce

Lord, make me chaste—but not yet.

—St. Augustine

A few months after I left the house and before my divorce was finalized, I started dating Bambi the Missile Maker.

That's not her real name, of course, but believe me, it's close enough. Bambi was a perpetually tan hardbody with towering blond hair who drove a white Corvette with vanity license plates and worked on a supersecret jet fighter for a defense contractor. She lived with a girlfriend in a cottage on the beach, drank white Zinfandel like it was water, and put pineapple on her pizza.

Bambi was ten years younger than I, had never been married, and was pretty well convinced she wouldn't make a good mother. She came from a fundamentalist family in the

Southwest with a military tradition and was a lieutenant in the Navy reserves.

We had absolutely nothing in common.

I had to do it, though. The relationship, if you could call it that, was too stereotypical to resist: a middle-aged divorced guy and a California beach bunny. Give me a break. Besides, it gave my two married buddies the vicarious thrill of a lifetime.

After Bambi and I stopped seeing each other—it didn't take long, thankfully—it occurred to me that she had never mentioned my divorce. Not once. I had made no secret of the fact that I was divorced with a young son, of course, but Bambi had never shown even the slightest curiosity about Alex or my relationship with him. And I never had even the slightest urge to bring the two of them together.

I don't know of any divorced dad who doesn't have a Bambi lurking somewhere in his postdivorce life. Dating and sexuality after divorce often seem like one long string of humiliating or just plain funny situations, especially when your kids get involved. Dating and sexuality are difficult enough subjects to master when you're single. It's doubly tough when you're single with children.

Easy Does It

Typically, divorced dads tend to respond to the prospect of seeing other women again by swinging between two extremes. This is almost a rite of passage for the newly divorced, and although most of us navigate it within a year or two, it can last much, much longer than that. During this confused and confusing period, divorced guys either act like monks, in effect giving up the opposite sex to devote all their time and attention to their kids, or they carry on like horny sixteen-year-olds, hitting the singles bars with a vengeance and jumping from one relationship—or bed—to another. Neither approach is healthy, of course, in every sense of the word, and both types of behavior spring from the same, divorce-induced pain.

The divorce experts don't offer much good advice on how to avoid falling into one of the two postbreakup dating patterns. When they do recommend a course of action, it can be so warm and fuzzy that it's ludicrous to a divorced dad. One of the funniest moments I had in researching this book, for example, was when I came across a well-meaning female divorce author who suggested that divorced fathers with hyperactive sexual urges replace their desire for one-night stands with "a lot of hugs." Needless to say, this is not the kind of advice a guy is going to embrace with a lot of enthusiasm (unless he's hugging his date).

Assuming that they don't enter into another relationship right away, most divorced men eventually will settle into a dating routine that hews pretty close to whatever practical advice the experts provide. That is, their social lives tend to be marked more by caution than anything else, an obvious reaction to the breakups of their marriages. And that's a good thing.

A divorce can shake anyone's self-esteem, and both you and your kids need a breather to collect yourselves and lay the foundations of your new life together as a "binuclear family." Besides, your ability to trust has taken a beating. You need to rebuild that as well. A divorced dad needs time to come to terms with what he's just gone through and so do his kids—who certainly don't need another rival for Dad's attention and affection at an extraordinarily vulnerable point in their relationship with him. With all the explaining and reassuring you have to do after divorce, you don't need to add the thorny subject of an immediate rival for mom as well.

Your kids' reaction when you start dating again will range from incomprehension to antagonism. Divorced dads with toddlers find that their little ones don't really understand the whole dating process. Art Edelstein's four-year-old son, for example, had no problem having daddy's friend stay over, but he did have difficulty comprehending why she had to go home in the morning.

Older kids, by contrast, can be very resentful, even ones just slightly older than the young Edelstein boy was when he had his close encounter in the hallway with Art's girl-friend. Daughters especially can be very possessive of their dad. One little seven-year-old girl, asked to sit in the back of the car when her dad brought a lady friend with them one day, plaintively cried out, "But I'm no longer the queen."

Says her father, with masterful understatement, "It takes an unusual partner to be able to deal with that, and some women are just put off by it. But that little kid and I have been through a lot together. She has a special place and that's just the way it is."

"I basically gave up trying to date when I have the kids because it's nearly impossible," adds Kevin, the divorced dad we met in an earlier chapter. "So instead I focus on the kids and we go out a lot. My girlfriend is okay with it; we don't have a hot and heavy relationship and she has kids as well, so she understands."

On the other hand, you don't want to live through your kid. It's way too easy to let them fill your emotional needs and neglect your social life. Granted, this is more of a prob-lem for custodial moms than for noncustodial dads, but it can happen to anybody.

Whatever your individual situation or the age of your chil-dren may be, it's a universally good idea to take it easy in the dating department at first. Go slow. Wait six months or a year. Otherwise, you may have to deal with an envious child or, even worse, waste a lot of time, money, and self-respect on somebody named Bambi.

Out of Sight, but Not out of Mind

For a few years after his divorce, a dad living in California had a long-term casual girlfriend who got to know his kids pretty well, but his relationship with the woman was never spelled out to his children. One night, the girlfriend asked his seven-and-a-half-year-old daughter how she would feel about Daddy having a girlfriend.

"It's too early!" the little girl cried.

It's very awkward for divorced dads to broach the subject of dating with their kids, no matter what the age. Most make an effort to keep casual relationships completely off their children's radar screen. That's the prudent course of action. Kids often act out like crazy with girlfriends. Why? Jealousy, fear that they'll lose you, or the illogical but tenacious dream they all have of seeing their parents back together again one day.

Besides, when your kids are ready to discuss your love life with you, they'll let you know.

A New York divorced dad made a point of not discussing his relationships with his daughters. One day he was in his kitchen making a snack with the oldest, a young teen.

"Why don't you ever go out?" she asked him.

"You are why," he answered. "I don't want to hurt your feelings."

"It won't hurt my feelings," his daughter countered. "Why don't you get a life?"

"It won't hurt your feelings?"

"No, it won't, and I can speak for the other girls too. We want you to be happy."

At that point this dad realized that his kids didn't want the responsibility of his happiness. They were telling him he had done a good job; they were secure in his love. So he came clean with his kid.

"I have gone out a lot, but I haven't discussed it with you," he admitted.

"Well, you can," she said.

But this dad still doesn't make a habit of introducing his daughters to everybody he takes out because he doesn't think it's fair.

"Doing that would just kind of give me the creeps," he

says. "I prefer to keep that part of my life separate until I'm serious about it."

He's right. You owe your kids that much at least. In the five years that I've been divorced, I have had several relationships but nothing serious. For that reason, Alex has met women I've dated exactly twice, each time because the logistics of picking up the woman and dropping Alex off at his mom's made it possible. Never because I planned to do it.

I'm an extreme example, but the advice you get in this area will be close to unanimous: *wait at least until a relationship is past the casual stage before introducing your new friend to your kids*. When the time comes, moreover, you must proceed with great care and pay close attention to maintaining good communication. Remember, that reconciliation fantasy lurks in the subconscious of every child of divorce, and even the potential of a serious relationship between you and another woman may spark additional acting out.

When is a relationship past the casual stage? That's your call. Radio psychologist and sex therapist Ann Christie defines it as when you've met "a potential mate." Whenever the time is right for you, it's imperative that you take care to explain, at your kids' comprehension level, what you're doing and why you're doing it, and that it doesn't threaten their relationship with you. I like the way this next dad handled the particular moment of truth in a divorced-dad's learning curve.

He had been dating a woman from Los Angeles, and the relationship was really moving along. So he decided it was time that she met his daughter. The dad invited her to come to New York on a weekend when he didn't have custody. He picked a day when his girl was on a play date, a time when he could stop by briefly to say hello and then leave.

The man introduced his girlfriend to his daughter, a preadolescent at the time, as "a friend of mine." Then he took his daughter aside and said, "I really like her and I want to see what you thought of her."

His daughter said, "Let me check." After a few minutes

with the girlfriend, his daughter took him aside and gave her approval. If she hadn't, this dad would have had a real dilemma on his hands but he says parenting must take precedence over his social life.

Should a little girl less than ten years old be given this kind of adult acknowledgment? Perhaps not in a nuclear family, or even in your divorced-dad household—maybe your situation is such that you feel uncomfortable having such adult exchanges with your child. I'll admit, this guy's kid sounds precocious as hell, but after all, she was a New Yorker.

Seriously, though, this girl was a child of divorce, and they're not like ordinary kids. The ones with good parents like hers invariably are tough, smart, and able to cope. Her father was saying to his daughter, in effect, "You are very important to me and this lady is very important to me. So I would like it if you approve of this person."

The great baseball pitcher Dizzy Dean once said, "If you can do it, then you ain't braggin'." As far as I know, this divorced dad is one of the fortunate few who has had no problems at all with his children about his social life.

At any rate, the divorced-dad parenting principle this man followed was quite sound. You should *introduce new people into your mutual life with your kids gradually*. This father picked a nonvisitation period to bring his daughter and his girlfriend together, but you will probably face that situation on one of your weekends. Many divorce experts advise that you continue to spend the bulk of your visitation time with your child and only slowly incorporate your new partner into the mutual history you share with your kids. Keep the initial get-togethers short. Some even suggest that, at first, you invite one of your kid's friends over as well, to minimize the chances that your child will feel competitive with your new friend.

Greg took that advice one step further and turned having the girlfriend over into a special event.

"We phased into it," he says. "The three of us would spend time together, and gradually increase the amount.

Then she started coming over for dinner. My son actually looked forward to that because we got to eat in the dining room instead of the kitchen, and we'd have hor d'ouevres, and things like that. So he was never really bothered by the situation."

Not all fathers are so lucky. After your marriage breaks up, your children fear that you will abandon them. That feeling will return when you begin a serious relationship with a woman, particularly if your child is a teenager when it happens. It is at that turbulent time of life that young men and women desperately need the steadying influence of a father in their life. Any threat to remove or diminish that presence, which a new love for you certainly represents, may create emotional problems.

The problem is, your kid is not going to put a sign up in his room that says, "I'm having difficulty accepting your girlfriend." In fact, his behavior may be calculated to drive you away. He may be so obnoxious to your new girlfriend or your fiancée that it almost seems he's trying to get you angry. Well, he is. But his bad attitude is a twisted sort of cry for help.

The only recourse you have in such a situation is that old divorced-dad standby: honesty. Be open and reassure your son, make him understand how special he remains to you, and underscore that your commitment to him has not wavered because there is once again a woman in your life.

Back in the Saddle Again

Every noncustodial dad eventually reaches the point where he's ready to face his social moment of truth. The psychological scars are healed, or at least healing. It's time to get back in circulation.

You know what I'm talking about. You might even be feeling it right now—the urge to merge. And you probably have only two tiny problems with that. First, you have no idea whom you're looking for. Second, you don't have a clue where to look.

Let's start with where to look. The answer depends on several things. Some divorced dads meet longtime girlfriends and even second wives at singles dances or through personal ads. Many singles, divorced or otherwise, prowl for partners at getaway weekends or at Club Med. If you're comfortable doing that, proceed cautiously. The odds of this method turning up someone with whom you can have a strong and healthy relationship are slim—I met Bambi on a getaway jaunt to Laughlin, Nevada, and my ex-wife on a singles weekend in Connecticut.

Many divorced dads find their new significant others in unlikely places, often with the aid of the most unlikely matchmakers. A divorced dad in L.A.'s San Fernando Valley, for example, literally found his new love in the laundry about three years ago. He walked into his dry cleaner one day just behind a very attractive woman about his own age. They made polite conversation and went their separate ways. The guy, a noncustodial divorced dad with two young kids, thought no more about it. But when he went back to pick up his clothes, the dry cleaner leaned close and whispered, "You know that woman who was here the last time really liked you. She keeps asking about you. And she's a divorced parent, just like you."

"Really?" the guy asked.

"Absolutely," said this father's very own commercial Cupid. "Should I ask her if I can give you her phone number?"

"Sure," the man said.

Next trip to the cleaner, the guy took home the woman's number along with his shirts.

It wasn't until months later that he found out he'd been set up: the dry cleaner had told *her* that the guy was asking about her, and she had only referred to the guy once, offhandedly noting that he seemed nice.

But the dry cleaner's instincts were impeccable; the couple hit it off and have been together ever since. And their di-

vorced friends keep bugging them to give them the dry
cleaner's address.

Shortly after the breakup of his marriage, Dean Hughson,
the online divorce expert, decided to get back in the dating
game. He had a lot of concerns—the threat of sexually trans-
mitted disease, whether he could perform, what to do if and
when his kids met his dates. But it was the 1990s, he figured,
so why not? He took an ad out in his local newspaper: "40-
year-old man, dream-maker, looking for women who appreciate men who are gentle and adventurous."

He received one hundred letters in thirty days. Women
doctors, women lawyers, waitresses, women with pictures.
He had thirty dates in thirty days, met a lot of interesting
people, and quickly learned they weren't very good at easing
his divorced-dad pain.

For one thing, many of these women lived a lot faster than
a guy who had been married for thirteen years. And when
these particular respondents discovered he had some money,
they wanted to help him spend it on weekends in Hawaii.
For another thing, Dean was still emotionally wounded,
which made him easy pickings for women who didn't want
a serious relationship.

In the end, though, he found a wonderful woman who
eventually became his second wife. But not through the clas-
sifieds. They were introduced by a friend.

*You are far more likely to meet someone suitable through friends
or by pursuing personal interests—going to the library, taking a
continuing education class—than through a personal ad.* Another
way divorced dads meet people is through groups of various
kinds, like group dates, which are sort of disguised match-
making events. You go out with a bunch of friends, who
bring other friends, and connections are made. At least in
these instances, you have someone else to talk to if things go
awry.

Another social resource for divorced dads, and it is an invaluable one, is Parents Without Partners (PWP), a national
organization with a chapter in virtually every major city in

the country. PWP is exactly what it sounds like, an organization dedicated to providing a connection between single
parents. Chapters hold dances, have field trips with kids, do
all sorts of great things.

Many churches and synagogues in America also have single parent groups. These are ideal ways to ease yourself back
onto the social calendar.

In 1957 twenty-five single parents met in a Greenwich
Village church basement in response to newspaper ads
placed by a noncustodial father and a custodial mother
and aimed at "Parents Without Partners." Today, PWP
has more than 85,000 members in more than five hundred chapters in the United States, Australia, West Ger-
many, Great Britain, and New Zealand.

One ritual you are certain to become far too familiar with
is the setup, the obligatory parade of blind dates and referrals
that every single person, but especially a divorced person,
has to endure. Everybody you know—your mother, your
mother's friend, your single friends, your married friends,
your female friends, your male friends, people whose names
you hardly remember—is going to act like your personal dating service and try to set you up at least once.

Usually these encounters lack chemistry of any kind, and
sometimes they are absolute torture. Especially since the prevailing custom is for you to make the initial phone call. There
isn't a more awkward way to meet someone than over the
phone, particularly when all you really know about the person is her name and number.

Setups by friends and relatives, however, also serve as an
automatic date-screening device for you, since your happy
helpers are usually very serious about matching you up with
somebody safe, or at least someone without any outstanding
warrants. So it's okay to accept this considerate but mis-

guided help until you get tired of it. To paraphrase an old joke, it probably won't help but it couldn't hurt. I'm in the midst of being set up as I write this chapter, in fact. Seems a mother of one of the kids on my soccer team knows someone, who has just called me to tell me she knows someone I might like.

Maybe I will and maybe I won't, but I'm skeptical. For one thing, the woman I'm to be set up with is a paralegal. Nothing wrong with that in general, but if my first marriage taught me anything, it's that it takes a rare breed of human to put up with a writer, and that exclusive group usually does not include left-brained people such as doctors, lawyers and business executives. People who don't know me well aren't likely to take that into account when setting me up with one of their friends.

Plus this potential date, fine person that she may be, is thirty-eight years old and has never wanted to get married, which sends my divorced-dad dating early warning system into a siren-screaming frenzy, because it means she may disagree with me on a fundamental issue: parenting. What's a divorced-dad dating early warning system? A foolproof detection method for when you are about to waste your time and money with someone who is not right for you and vice versa. Which brings us to who you should be looking for.

She Said, "It Sounds Creepy"; I Said, "So Long"

When you're a single parent, you're like a walking lie detector on dates, because almost nothing is as revealing of a woman's true character as her attitudes on marriage and children. As many divorced dads discover, it's almost impossible not to bring up this subject on a first date, usually right away, and it's equally impossible for your companion to hide her feelings on the subject. Perhaps one-third of the available single women you meet don't really want to date someone with a child. You'll know immediately one way or another. These ladies may just want to have fun, like Dean Hughson's unappealing dates, or they'll "Bambi" the subject, avoiding or deflecting discussion about it at all costs. (Most of these women tend to be in their early thirties or younger. You really can't blame them. Kids are an awe-inspiring responsibility, especially to people who have never had any, and older women have more experience with and are more accepting of that kind of responsibility.)

Another third will ooh and aah about your parenthood, and when or if they meet your children will make extraordinary efforts to get your kids to like them. These women are way too eager to please. In fact, there's a whole subsection of humanity out there desperately trying to fill the void in their lives by "finding" a family.

The remaining section of the available dating pool will strike just the right balance of interest in your situation and your children, and have the sensitivity not to force anything. Not surprisingly, this group includes single mothers. Inevitably, you will have more in common with somebody who shares such life-changing experiences as parenting and divorce.

In any event, don't saunter out into the social world with such lofty expectations that a goddess couldn't satisfy you. Divorced dads sometimes set their hopes too high for relationships or have impossible-to-meet standards, often as a defense mechanism, but sometimes just because they're being unrealistic. I used to have what I call "red flags" that alerted me I was with a person I should reject. Since most of these tipoffs were petty and the others aren't relevant at the beginning of a relationship (I automatically eliminated a woman if she said she didn't like baseball, for example), I did a lot more red flag waving than dating. Loosen up. Meeting new people can be fun if you don't treat every encounter as a prenuptial trial.

Besides, you're not the only one taking stock, you know. A guy like you is going to be under extraordinary scrutiny no matter whom you go out with, since your erstwhile part-

ners will be measuring you against all the divorced-dad ster-
eotypes. Involved single fathers can be irresistibly sexy to
some women (they are, by definition, "sensitive" guys), but
they are also suspect for a number of reasons. Before you can
start a relationship, you're going to have to answer some
questions, spoken or intimated.

Women will want to know how attached you are to your
ex-wife, and they won't understand your relationship with
your former spouse if it's anything other than totally hostile.
The culture still thinks of divorce as an endless, vicious war,
and if you have a cooperative relationship with your ex-wife,
your potential girlfriends are going to be suspicious at best
and insulting at worst. When I told someone on our first date
about my relationship with my ex and that I occasionally take
Alex to the doctor or to school if his mother is too busy to
do so, the woman said she thought that sounded "creepy."
The date couldn't have ended fast enough for me.

Two other questions that will be running through their
heads as they smile at you over their Chablis are: How connected is he to his kid? Will he put his kid before me? Personally, I'd answer "very" and "yes" to those queries, but
every divorced dad is different.

Your point of view about your failed marriage will be very
revealing to women, because they're looking for maturity.
They want to know if you learned something or if you're a
bad risk. Are you still angry? They won't like that. (Do not
under any circumstance call your ex-wife names in front of
your dates or girlfriends. You might as well wear a sign that
says "self-centered bastard" if you do.)

Lastly, don't be offended if, when you're considering making a commitment, she asks you about your finances. Your
partner is going to want to know about your alimony and
child support payments. It's common knowledge, despite the
media's characteristic myopia on the topic, that fathers as
well as mothers are often impoverished by divorce. In many
states, second wives' income is included when the government calculates a remarried divorced dad's child support to

his first wife. In California, in fact, the practice has sparked a fierce firefight in the uncivil war, with second wives and ex-wives in the Golden State organizing, petitioning, and attacking each other.

Whomever you date and however you go about finding them, please keep one thing uppermost in your mind: your children are watching. They will take their cues on how to behave in relationships and dating from you just like they learn how to do everything else. Never forget that your primary job as a parent is to set an example.

So set a good one. And be careful out there.

CHAPTER 9

―――――◆―――――

Step Lightly:
Divorced Dads and Remarriage

It's like déjà vu all over again.

—YOGI BERRA

About two years after we divorced, my ex-wife started dating a guy—let's call him Danny—who began talking about marriage on their first date. As their relationship progressed, Danny, divorced with no children, spent a lot of time rhapsodizing about what a wonderful life he and my ex and Alex were going to have. Danny badly wanted to be a father, he said. In fact, he had practiced his parenting techniques on his two nieces. He was fully prepared, he assured my ex, to work with me for Alex's benefit.

Very nice. Except that when he made these vows, Danny and my ex-wife had been dating for two months at most.

And he didn't have a clue what I was like. He hadn't even met me yet.

It wasn't long before Danny starting making plans for his soon-to-be family. They would all move up north when his company reassigned him. After that, they would move back to his native Midwest. Then they didn't know what they were going to do.

Each new decision was announced to me by my ex. It drove me crazy; I needed all my inner resources just to keep from screaming at her. The thought of losing Alex (that's how I saw it) ripped me apart. And the constantly changing nature of their plans kept me in turmoil. Plus, there was something about Danny that just wasn't right. But I couldn't be sure my concerns about him weren't just jealousy in disguise.

Alex, for his part, loved to play with Danny. Soon, however, he started being difficult whenever his mother's boyfriend tried to discipline him. He also became concerned about getting my approval of Danny. I told my son that Danny seemed like a nice guy, and if he was good to Mommy and Alex, that was okay with me. Later I learned that Danny had been verbally very rough with Alex on a couple of occasions, and in fact had come close to being abusive. I didn't have to be Sherlock Holmes to realize that Alex's change in attitude toward Danny occurred at around the same time.

And I *still* hadn't met the guy. Then one day about four months after all of this started, I received a call at work.

"Jack, this is Danny," a confident voice on the other end of the phone said. "I just want you to know that I know you are Alex's dad and I have no intention of keeping you from seeing your son. Be assured that when he's with me I'll be a good parent to him. I'm sure we can cooperate on disciplining him and together we can raise him right."

I mean, this was our first conversation. You'd think a future stepfather would at least try to be a little circumspect in his initial encounter with the biological father. But Danny's declaration seemed almost calculated to enrage me. That call reaffirmed my belief that he was a lot more in love with the idea of having a family than he was with my ex-wife.

Eventually, thank heaven, my ex-wife broke up with Danny, in no small measure because of his unrelenting pressure to create an instant family. We had a postmortem on the relationship, and I discovered that she had shared my misgivings about the relationship almost from the start.

Today more than 5 million married couples have stepchildren living with them and by the year 2000, it is predicted that 50 percent of the population of the U.S. will be a member of a "blended" family.

Danny was the closest I've come so far to having to deal with a stepfather, and if I never get any closer that will be just fine with me. But the choice isn't mine, and anyway, Alex is just as likely to have a stepmother some day. Seven out of every ten divorced American men and women remarry, and 40 percent of those unions involve stepchildren. In fact, more than one thousand new stepfamilies are created in the United States every day.

So the odds are fairly good that either you or your ex-wife will remarry. Unfortunately there's also a good chance that a second marriage will turn out just like the first, since more second marriages than first marriages fail: 60 percent versus 40 percent. Should one or both of you re-up for a tour of marital duty, you are going to find yourself exactly where I was during the Danny saga, where divorced dads usually find themselves when it comes to postdivorce parenting resources: totally on your own.

"Care for an Apple, Dearie?"

The call to the Stepfamily Foundation's counseling hotline was frantic. Although more of the foundation's clients are men than women, this caller was female, engaged to a non-custodial divorced dad. Her fiancé's two sons had just called him and said, "If you marry her, you'll never see us again."

Of course, this wasn't his kids talking to him, this was his ex-wife calling through the kids. The man was devastated, completely at a loss about how to handle this terrible threat. So his girlfriend went to the phone to get some help.

Shrinks, social scientists, divorce counselors, and the politically correct have a wonderful phrase for stepfamilies: "blended." Sounds so nice and smooth, doesn't it? Hardly. Remarriage is like going through the divorce all over again, for parents and their children. All the old feelings resurface and start working that old black magic. In addition, the new players in the drama can be threats, accidentally or not, direct or indirect, to the relationship between the kids and their biological parents. So, just as in the divorce, everybody involved in the creation of a blended (ugh) family is deeply affected. However, just as with divorce, the majority of resources available to parents on both sides of the step-fence focus on stepmothers.

For once, the reason behind this isn't the Tender Years Doctrine, although it does have its origins in very old ideas. The wicked stepmother is one of the most enduring characters in Western myths and fairy tales. Not coincidentally, the characters who mess with old women in these fables often discover to their dismay that she is literally a witch. This is not surprising, since most of the tellers of these tales were old women themselves, so it was in their best interests to make people (especially pretty young girls) respectfully wary of crones.

Today stories about malevolent second wives still permeate books, TV, and films. The persistence of the wicked stepmother stereotype is a factor in research indicating that among all children who become part of stepfamilies, girls whose fathers have remarried have the most trouble adjusting. There are apparently a lot of little girls out there who see themselves as Cinderella.

Many times ex-wives and stepmothers don't get along spectacularly. Often women have a more difficult time emotionally with the idea of a new wife than men have with the idea of the former spouse finding a new husband. (If you're paying alimony, you might actually be hoping for it.) Most experts believe this difference is caused by women's nurturing instincts, which are more directly threatened when a stepmother enters the picture.

Even when there isn't outright hostility between the former and current wives, females can react strongly to the other woman. "Ms. Enlightenment," for example, is one divorced custodial mom's sarcastic nickname for her husband's new wife. But at least that mom didn't drag her ex-husband into the fray, which is what befell Adam, the divorced dad we met earlier.

Adam and his second wife returned to the Northwest to attend his daughter's high school graduation. After the ceremony, they stopped by his ex-wife's house. She sat them down in the living room and then, to Adam and his wife's slack-jawed amazement, brought out wedding pictures from Adam's first marriage and spent the next forty-five minutes reliving the old days photo by photo.

Somehow Adam's second wife kept a poker face through the whole ordeal. But the instant the two of them walked out of the house, she declared, "I will never see that bitch again."

Stepfathers, we are told, are not usually hostile to the biological father and don't criticize the divorced dad's methods or style. This may be true in the main (Adam got along just fine with his ex-wife's two subsequent husbands), but it is far from universal. Nevertheless, as my close encounter with Danny illustrates, good men do face some potentially painful challenges when their ex-wives find a new Mr. Right.

Sorry, Only One to a Customer

Leslie Pam and Ann Christie say by far the biggest problems they hear about from divorced parents who call their radio show are conflicts with or problems adjusting to their ex-spouse's new mate. One morning, for example, the divorced dad of an eight-year-old boy called the radio show in tears.

"My son is calling his stepfather Daddy," the man sobbed.

Though sociologists and psychologists may minimize the chances of kids encountering an "evil stepfather"—they are relatively rare (except in, you guessed it, the movies and the media)—that doesn't mean divorced dads have no reason to worry. One of the biggest threats is the very one the caller to the radio show faced, an attempt by a stepfather to take the place of the biological father. In the Binuclear Study done by Constance Ahrons, most women said they were like friends to their stepkids. Most men, on the other hand, described their relationship with their stepkids as *parental*. In fact, one-third of the stepfathers in Ahrons's study said their stepkids called them Dad, compared to only 12 percent of stepmothers who were called Mom by their new husband's kids. Tellingly, the divorced fathers who had to share the Dad moniker with their kids' stepfather were those who were least involved with their children.

A woman I know answered a phone call from her nephew's biological father. The parents had been divorced since the boy was four. Not thinking, she told her nephew his "father" had called. He assumed she meant his stepdad, who in actuality had raised the young man. The biological father, on the other hand, had seen the boy only a few times over the years. Suddenly the real dad was wanting to be a part of his son's life again. Although he was able to get somewhat close to his son again, he never regained the position of Dad. That position had been well filled by the stepdad. To this day, the son calls his biological father by his first name and his stepfather Dad.

When women remarry, they often want their new man to replace the old one in their children's eyes. So they may encourage the kids to call their stepfather Daddy. They might even suggest that the stepfather adopt the kids because "it will be better for them." Some women even enroll the children in school under the stepfather's last name. Also, some new fathers may have a strong urge to parent and, like Danny, get a little too carried away. They'll often encourage Mom to help them replace the biological dad.

Your interaction with your ex-wife doesn't need to be all that hostile for any of these situations to arise either, because women are extremely good at denying, even to themselves, that their ex-husbands have any enduring interest in being parents. Cedars-Sinai psychologist Dr. Frank Williams believes that the actions most likely to reignite conflict between two divorced parents are mothers encouraging their children to address stepfathers or boyfriends as Daddy and placing the kids in school under a stepfather's last name.

They ought to be cause for conflict. Given the danger to kids' emotional well-being from open warfare between their parents, there are very few instances when it's in a divorced dad's interest to go on the attack, but those are two of them. You must not under any circumstances give in to these changes, or others like them, in your relationship with your children. That includes any and all attempts to change your child's last name. They are slippery slopes down which you will surely fall, and in the end you will lose your kids.

Follow the advice of experts and *suggest that your ex encourage your children to think of their stepfather as an addition to their circle of caring adults, rather than a replacement dad.* That's a whole lot different than agreeing, in effect, to give up your parenthood. And don't shy away from using legal threats if you must—stepparents do not have the rights you do.

Make it clear to the stepdad and your ex-wife that while you have no problems with sharing child-rearing duties, you neither need nor welcome a third parent. You and you alone are your child's father, and you should be firm in conveying the message that your child should not be encouraged for any reason to call anyone but you Daddy.

What's Good for the Goose . . .

Since you also are likely to remarry sooner or later, chances are you'll find yourself in the position of stepfather. So you'd better learn how it feels from the other side too.

Five years ago, if you had asked Steve if he loved his two stepdaughters, he would have enthusiastically answered yes. Now he has to pause. Well, he'll say, he is concerned for their welfare. Steve and his wife, Betty (it's his first marriage, her second), have tried hard to parent wisely in their five years of marriage. They even see a therapist for that purpose. But the girls' biological father, Bob, refuses to cooperate at all with his ex and her new husband.

Last year, at Bob's urging, the girls, both teenagers, took Steve and their mother to court. They made all sorts of accusations about Betty being an unfit mother, and the judge took custody away from her and gave it to Bob.

At their father's, the girls had to clean the house every other week, but aside from that chore, there didn't appear to be much parenting going on. The younger began smoking, then doing drugs, then skipping school. She had done none of those things when she lived with Steve and Betty.

Within six months the girl moved back in with her mother and stepfather. The older would dearly love to, but that would mean giving up the car her paternal grandparents bought for her after the custody trial.

Both his stepdaughters treat Steve with such contempt that his parenting decisions have to be delivered by Betty or the girls won't obey them. And the younger remains a nightmare child, throwing screaming tantrums at every opportunity.

On top of all this, Steve is very conscious of how precarious his position as a stepdad with two teenage stepdaughters is in the ever-vigilant eyes of the social system. He refuses to be alone with either of the girls for any length of time, because it would take only one vague accusation of abuse to ruin his life. In fact he feels compelled to leave his own house when his stepdaughters are home and his wife is out running errands. During those periods Steve walks around the neighborhood until Betty comes home, and he makes sure the neighbors see him.

A stepparent is appropriately named, because he or she gets stepped on all the time. The challenges are larger, the intensity greater, the roiling emotional sea you have to sail across wilder and more dangerous, perhaps, than the one you survived during your divorce.

Stepparents, it seems, are damned if they do and damned if they don't.

Stepdad's a good guy? Then his stepkids may be curt with him because otherwise they'd feel disloyal to their biological dad. Stepdad isn't coming across as a good guy? Now the stepkids will really give it to him—major yelling, fighting, tantrum-throwing and general chaos. In either case, the stepkids are not going to put up with being told what to do by the likes of him, whether it's sitting straight at the table, cleaning up their rooms or anything else And, of course, there's always the lurking presence of that special stepfamily demon, jealousy. The kids may feel that the new mate will steal Mommy away from them just as divorce stole their Daddy. Besides, with him around, how are the kids ever going to get Mommy and Daddy back together again?

It would take a separate book to cover every aspect of being a stepdad, and a fat book at that. In fact, there are many such books already. There are as many stepparenting experts, organizations, and self-help groups for stepfamilies as there are experts, organizations, and self-help groups for divorced women. (My nominee for best step-group name, by the way, has to be Duet Again, headquartered in Des Moines, Iowa.)

Just as in divorce, there are basics to stepparenting that everybody can learn, and universal challenges that must be met no matter what your individual circumstance may be. So if you find the wedding band is on the other finger and you're the one becoming a stepparent, here are a few pointers that can help:

• *Don't expect the new family to be like a nuclear family.* Everybody has differences; embrace them.

• *Work with your stepkids' biological parent as an ally, not a competitor, if at all possible.* Create what John and Emily Visher, the couple that co-founded the Stepfamily Association of America in the late 1970s, call a "family coalition." This doesn't mean you have to be their dad's buddy or make him a part of your family. Most relationships between biological fathers and stepfathers are cordial but not close. Best bet: treat it as a working relationship. And if you're like most guys, you'll be reluctant to criticize your stepkids' dad in front of them. Some experts don't see anything wrong with discussing a biological father's shortcomings with stepchildren, although most recommend that you don't get into that quagmire. I agree with the majority: leave your opinions of their dad out of your relationship with your stepkids. You, better than most, should understand how unfair and slanderous other people's perceptions of a noncustodial dad can be.

• *Establish new traditions* for your "blended" family the same way you make a mutual history or unique holiday tradition when you're divorced. Do something different from the way everybody's previous family did it, do it together, and keep doing it.

• *Go slow.* The sheer weight of all the transformations stepfamilies go through can sink even the best intentions. Many stepdads move too fast in trying to put their own personal fathering stamp on the new family. That just creates resentment. Take it easy, and evolve into your new situation gradually.

• *Get involved.* This is another divorced-dad principle you can apply to stepparenting. Get involved in your stepkids' lives outside the home. Be aware, however, that you're going to get even less support from society than you do as a noncustodial divorced dad, if that's possible. Arguments over a stepparent's interaction with the stepchildren—almost always because the stepparent wants to be more involved—are a primary source of disagreement among remarried couples.

• *Respect your ex.* When you decide to rehitch, it's important that you let your ex-wife know as soon as possible that you plan to remarry. Playing games like letting her find out from your kid is going to backfire for all the obvious reasons. You're going to have enough on your plate as a blended kind of guy without having to deal with bitterness and resentment from your former spouse.

• *Don't emotionally ignore your new wife.* By now you should be quite good at being sensitive; if not, brother, you are in for a wild ride. Seriously, though, carefully consider your new love's feelings toward your "old" family. Your time with your kids may be wonderful for you, but it is sure to be a strain for her, at least to some degree. Noncustodial visits are an ordeal for many second wives. Also be alert to embarrassing or humiliating situations, like the one Adam and his new wife endured. You may not be able to prevent them, but you can at least provide emotional support for your new wife. Do not, under any circumstances, minimize her feelings about the stresses she must confront.

• *Accept changes in the visitation schedule.* Inevitably, remarriage means that someone sooner or later is going to broach the subject of changing the visitation setup. No one should rush into any such change, obviously, but be prepared to do it if a new visitation schedule makes sense. Be aware, however, that your kids may feel even more threatened by such change, since it signals yet another area where they have no control over what happens to them. Finally, it's a good idea not to formally change custody for the first eighteen months to two years after a remarriage.

The Stepfamily Foundation Excellent Eight

The Stepfamily Foundation, one of the biggest and oldest self-help resources for "blended" moms, dads, and kids, offers ten tips for men "in step," which it defines quite broadly as single and divorced fathers who have remarried or are in a steady relationship with a woman who also has her own children. Two of these recommendations are similar to topics we have already discussed—don't be a Disneyland Dad, and learn how to do "mothering" things like cooking. The remaining eight, however, are sound and savvy additional suggestions:

1. *The stepfather cannot function like the biological father* He can, however, partner with his wife and jointly run the household with "couple power." In time a stepfather should also take on the role of teacher. This is what Steven has done in his stepfamily and, although he's enduring the trials of Job right now, his stepdaughters will almost certainly thank him when their turbulent teens are over.

2. *Structuring the household should be a shared task.* Each member of the household, including the children, should have clearly defined duties and responsibilities—chores, as we've seen, may be a parent's most effective tool for sharing, teaching, disciplining, and reassuring.

3. *The couple must discuss and agree on when, how, and why to exercise discipline in the household.* The foundation suggests that the biological parent discipline and the stepparent remind. Step-expert Kevin Leman recommends that steparents adopt the phrase "relationships before rules" as a guideline. One step-couple, for example, made a list of the rules of their new household and presented it to their children for discussion. The rules included simple how-to-get-along requirements as well as an admonishment that the adults always had the final say. This couple, which claims to have had remarkably little trouble with disciplining their "blended" brood, lets the biological parent take the lead, with the stepparent present to underscore that both adults share authority.

4. *Don't overdiscipline your stepkids.* This is the most frequent criticism of stepdads and it should be, because being too tough never works. The foundation vividly describes how a biological mother responds when a stepdad too enthusiastically refuses to spare the rod, saying it brings out the "mama bear protecting her young from the outsider syndrome."

5. *Predictability and organization create intimacy.* When there is a day-to-day structure in the home, a set of well-understood and reasonable family rules, the potential for conflict is minimized and kids adjust much better. So do their parents.

6. *Unrealistic expectations beget rejections and resentments.* There is no blueprint for a nonnuclear family. Be a student of alternative family lifestyles and don't expect too much of anybody, especially yourself.

7. *Be aware of the conflict between sexual and biological pulls in stepfamily relationships.* This means that your desire to be with your new wife may conflict with your desire to make your kids happy. Don't let your loyalties to your biological kids and your sexual relationship with your new wife collide. Easier said than done, of course, but you can manage if you're alert to the possible conflict.

8. *Guard your sense of humor and use it.* Self-explanatory.

The Roller Coaster Rolls Again

Dean Hughson still has trouble with his fifteen-year-old daughter. She'll say things like "we don't like that," meaning her and her mother. Dean believes the problems he has had and continues to have with his oldest daughter, and her almost ferocious alliance with her mother, stem from his remarriage.

When Dean and his first wife sat down with their lawyers to discuss custody, it looked as if he was going to have as smooth a divorce as one could hope for. His ex suggested joint custody and a mutual declaration that each knew the other was a good parent and wanted the ex-spouse to be fully involved in raising the kids.

"Take it, take it," his attorney advised. "That's incredible."

Four attorneys, accountants, a court reporter, and the Hughsons had battled for four days over the disposition of the couple's assets. It took five minutes to decide about their children. Dean's attorney was doing cartwheels.

"Most people spend hundreds of thousands of dollars to get this," the attorney exulted. Dean didn't care. He just wanted the pain to be over.

And it was—for a while. Dean's divorced-dad life began well enough. Every two weeks his kids would fly to Kansas City to be with him; every two weeks he'd fly to Arizona to be with them. But then everything changed. Dean got married again.

One day, not long after his wedding, he was handed a summons accusing him of abusing his children. His wife was suing for sole custody, claiming that he spoke "like a walrus," whatever that means, and scared her children and drove his car in a drunken and dangerous fashion.

A bitter court battle and $100,000 later, Dean was able to bury those ridiculous and heinous charges. But in the process, he found that his relationship with his oldest daughter, then ten years old, had deteriorated. Her mother had shared every agonizing moment of their divorce with their daughter, making her read court papers, that kind of thing. In effect, this poor little girl was led to believe that she was divorcing her daddy too.

The remarriage fanned this flame into an inferno. This was, after all, a little girl who had dreams about her parents meeting on the *Love Boat* and remarrying. When it was clear the boat was never going to sail, it hurt. Plenty. She also was angry at Dad's remarriage because it destroyed another fantasy she had: that her father would never remarry and she would move in and take care of him.

Emotionally, kids get knocked around the most by remarriage. They feel out of control, rejected, unwanted. Their most cherished hope, that their parents will reunite, is shattered with a terrible finality. Adding insult to injury, they are often asked to accept stepbrothers and stepsisters into their lives at the same time—more competition for Mommy's and Daddy's attention. Even worse, the remarriage of a parent brings back a child's anxieties from the divorce. The child may feel that showing affection to the stepparent is betraying the biological parent and so will act out that feeling by resisting the "new" parent, often with undisguised hostility.

Small wonder, then, that children in one-parent families generally fare better than those in blended families. In this case, in fact, that misleadingly gentle euphemism is right on the mark: in many ways that are very real to them, children pushed into a stepfamily are indeed put through a blender.

You can no more protect your kids from the consequences of remarriage than you could protect them from the aftereffects of divorce. But you can make the transition easier.

• *Tell kids about the impending remarriage as soon as possible*, and give them as much time as you can to get used to their soon-to-be stepparent. As far as the wedding ceremony is concerned, the experts are dramatically split on whether kids should be given special roles to play in the remarriage of a parent.

When Jeff remarried he decided to include his son Billy in the plans and the ceremony. "He was totally into it," says Jeff, "and it gave him a little finality about his mother and me. We also took him with us when we went to look at places to hold the reception. We showed him the church and the place we were going to get our tuxedos. He was great at the wedding."

My suggestion: go with your gut instinct, but in general, you don't want to rub a kid's nose in it. If you remarry, it may be wisest to let your kids be honored guests at the wedding rather than drag them into the proceedings.

• *Soothe their anxieties* by reminding them over and over how special they are to you, whether you are the one remarrying or it's their mother who is taking a new husband. Tell your kids firmly and as often as necessary that they are your first children and nobody can ever take that away from them. They will always occupy a separate and special place in your life. You must make clear to them that they will not be abandoned. And reassure them that their other biological parent still loves them too—if possible, work with your ex on this.

• *Don't expect miracles.* It takes time to "blend." They don't have to be bosom buddies with their new mommy right away. Let them know it's all right to ease into the new relationships.

CHAPTER 10

◆

The Ex Files:
Custodial Moms' Point of View

The safest course is to be as understanding as possible, and, where our understanding fails, to call charity to its aid.

—Laura Ingalls Wilder

With the unshakable self-assurance of the truly naive, I agreed to stay at my ex-wife's townhouse for two days while she was in Denver on a business trip. My mission: to take care of Sheba, the aging toy poodle with an attitude and a skin condition that made her smell like a very small toxic waste dump; Keesha, the frisky four-month-old Keeshond who had yet to grasp the finer points of being housebroken; and Alex.

I figured it was in my self-interest. I would get to spend

two unscheduled days with Alex, and the dogs wouldn't have to be put in a kennel. Relentlessly, my ex drilled me on my major responsibilities: feed the dogs, take them out, take care of the kid, and don't stain the carpets. No sweat. I could single-parent as well as she could. Off she went to the Rockies.

After work, I picked up Alex at his grandparents and we drove home. I was relaxed, confident, utterly sure of my ability. I opened the door.

Keesha had broken free of the gate that kept her from destroying the rest of the house and was leaping madly about, spraying yellow doggy joy juice all over the kitchen floor, her food dish, a nearby plant, and, within a few seconds, my brand-new, $150 tailored shirt. Sheba, the mutant poodle from hell, jumped to the top of my ex-wife's leather couch and growled at everybody, dropping sticky, impossible-to-remove doggy drool all over the couch.

Alex, embracing the chaos with enthusiasm, ran around the house screaming an obscene lyric from a Green Day song at the top of his lungs and waving around a large gray plastic sword—which almost immediately smashed into one of my ex's favorite vases, shattering it. I tripped over a large dog bone and fell nose-first onto the living room floor, from which vantage point I noticed that the carpet was newly stained in about a dozen different places.

After cleaning up (it took a whole roll of extra-strength Brawny paper towels), it was dinnertime. Keesha ate her food, then ate the poodle's food. The poodle jumped on Keesha's head. Alex ate his cheeseburger without taking the wrapper off. Keesha stole some of his French fries. He yelled. Keesha barked. The poodle glared. I spilled coffee on the kitchen floor.

After cleaning up (another roll of Brawny), it was upstairs for Alex's bath and then bedtime. Keesha tried to drink the bathwater. Then she chewed on one of my ex's shoes. Alex threw his action toys in and out of the tub, spraying dirty water everywhere. Keesha, chased away from the ex's shoes, started gnawing on mine. Downstairs, meanwhile, the poodle was piddling in the middle of the living room. After cleaning up, I fell into an uneasy sleep on my ex's bed.

At dawn, I got up and staggered downstairs to discover that Keesha had completely demolished the gate and deposited yellow doggy joy juice everywhere. I didn't know where Sheba was, but I could smell her. Alex played catch with his waffles, unsuccessfully. They splattered all over the kitchen.

After cleaning up (we were now almost out of Brawny), I rushed upstairs to take a shower. I'd barely gotten wet when the doorbell rang. Every living thing in the house started screeching. I rushed downstairs with a towel awkwardly wrapped around me and cracked open the door to find Flora, the cleaning lady, standing there with an embarrassed smile on her face. My ex had forgotten to tell me that Flora was coming that morning.

Eventually I fed Alex, found the spare gate and confined the Keeshond, located the poodle, and got dressed for work. Before I left the house to take Alex to his grandparents, I asked Flora if there was anything she could do about the stains on the carpet.

There wasn't.

My ex-wife called me at the office before she left Denver.

"How did it go?" she asked.

"Great! No problem," I said. "But you're going to need a lot more Brawny."

Side Unseen

In our zeal to see justice done, we divorced dads too often ignore the other, equally valid reality that single moms face some pretty huge challenges themselves. We forget there's always another side to any story.

Kathy should be having the time of her life. Her career as an actress is taking off, she's a regular on one of the most popular TV shows in America, and she's getting offers from all over. But behind the camera she has to deal with the non-custodial divorced dad from hell. Among many other faults, her ex-husband makes a point of embroiling their little six year-old boy in their affairs, telling him that "Mommy still loves me, you know. Go home and tell Mommy to come back to me."

Susan's ex-husband deliberately and systematically set out to bankrupt her, then used her precarious financial position as evidence against her in custody court and won sole custody of their kids.

Dina's alcoholic ex-husband delighted in badmouthing her in front of their children and then took their fifteen-year-old son down to Tijuana, Mexico, for a weekend drinking binge. Plus he maxed out the credit cards.

Jim's dad harbors a profound contempt for his ex-wife, Paula, and makes a persistent and explicit effort to recruit his son to that point of view. He does this despite showing no affinity for his son or any interest whatsoever in being a fully involved father.

Justin, a playful nine-year-old with big blue saucer eyes and sandy blond hair, says things are going okay for him and his mom, Abby. But, he adds, "I really miss my dad." The boy's father lives two states away and, despite assurances from Abby that she'll accept collect calls from him anytime, he never telephones his son. Asked what she needs most from her ex-husband, Abby says, "Only that he get involved."

If we divorced dads expect our case to be heard fairly and evaluated objectively, we must admit there are jerks aplenty on our side of the divorce settlement. Yet we are too often blinded by our own pain. The biggest problem I had while writing this book was getting guys to stop telling me their horror stories and stick to the purpose of the interview. No matter how many times I would steer a divorced dad back to his parenting success stories, sooner or later he would always jump back to moaning about how unfair his lot was and how rotten the system is to good men.

Sure it is. Most of us have been shafted by the courts or our former spouses at one time or another, and some of us have been figuratively beaten up by both at regular intervals. That's why I wrote this book. That doesn't mean, however, that we're completely blameless.

If you take the time to understand your ex-wife's reality, she's far more likely to understand yours. Indeed, the point of view expressed by Kathryn Gibson in the epigraph to this chapter is far more common than one might believe. More than half (52 percent) of the respondents to the Fathers Resource Center reader survey were women. The fact that so many moms took the time to answer a survey in a newsletter for fathers vividly illustrates that the other side is ready to talk peace in the uncivil war any time we are. In the end, though, the best reason for developing empathy for your ex-wife's life is that your kids will thank you for it.

There are four ways you can do this, although none of them is without cost, emotional or otherwise:

1. Respect and support your former spouse.
2. Compliment her on how well she's doing as a mother from time to time.
3. Fight to convince her of her own self-interest.
4. Unless you really are being unfairly squeezed, do not begrudge the money you give her.

These ideas require some explaining, I know. Let's begin with the first: respect and support your ex-wife. What really makes this vital is your enduring role as a teacher by example to your kids. They will look to you and they will imitate you—not just now, when they're kids, but throughout their lives. This is particularly true, by the way, if you have a seven- or eight-year-old son, since this is the developmental age at which boys consciously seek to emulate their fathers.

So if you respect their mother, they have a positive reference point for their own relationships later on. By showing respect I mean that you are civil and courteous to her. Civility in turn minimizes conflict and maximizes the potential for effective co-parenting, which also makes it harder for the kids to manipulate the two of you.

Respecting your former spouse means more than just being courteous to her, however. It also means respecting her right to have a private life. Do not pump your children for information about what their mother does in her home. Don't be implicitly critical. "Oh, sure," you might say to your kids in jest, "of course she had two dates last weekend. She oughta give it a rest once in a while." Serious or not, that's a dig, and kids of divorce have ultrasensitive radar when it comes to detecting barbs.

But here's an even more shocking suggestion: take respect one step further and actually be proactively supportive of your ex-wife. Applaud her successes. Help her in her career if you can. (I frequently help my ex-wife with business copywriting, and she, in turn, has made me several thousand dollars in the stock market.) Again, this is a positive example for your kids and an olive branch that most single women will accept, although they may grumble about it at first because they may not trust your motives.

The second suggestion is to compliment your ex-wife on her parenting. If you acknowledge her contributions to your kids' upbringing, you'll be amazed at how much smoother your relationship with her can be. Women are not used to their former spouses doing anything but complaining.

Don't be hypocritical and say what you don't feel. But in truth, most single mothers do a terrific job of child-rearing under very difficult circumstances. Give the woman her due, and you're likely to enjoy a refreshing reduction in the nastiness level of your relationship, which will, naturally, benefit your kids tremendously. This also gives your children a wonderful example of positive intergender relations, something none of us sees often enough.

Acknowledging your ex-wife's ability to parent, therefore, sends the signal that you do think about child-rearing—a lot—and you take it seriously. But put your money where your compliments are; if she has a good idea, go ahead and incorporate it into your own parenting policy.

A single mom I know shared a tip with me that she and her ex both use frequently. She keeps timers all over the house and has her two boys, aged nine and seven, set them whenever they begin an activity. If they want to play video games, for example, she tells them, "Okay, but just for thirty minutes—set the timer." And if they falter and need a time-out (every modern parent's best friend), she tells them, "in your room for a ten-minute time-out. Set the timer."

By using this method, you can avoid a lot of common parent/kid miscommunication, like having to tell them to turn off the TV four times before they actually do it. When they're being punished, they know the duration, and they are more willing to endure it without a fight.

The next recommendation for developing empathy for your ex is to try to make her see her self-interest more clearly, and then help her act on that realization. The more she allows you to take the kids to the doctor, baby-sit for them when she has a date, and so on, the more freedom she will have to pursue her own dreams. When you're a single mom, just being able to go to a movie rated higher than PG is like a gift from God.

Good men can be invaluable in loosening the screws that tighten around their ex-wives' lives. That's why, in the earliest years of the fathers' rights movements, feminists actually embraced the concept of joint physical custody.

Researcher Sanford Braver found that most dads wanted to be highly involved with their children, and those fathers who continued to feel needed and appreciated as parents never disengaged from their children. Those who were "disenfranchised," however, who felt that their relationship with their child was completely out of their control, who no longer had the fundamental right to involve themselves in their child's life, were the dads who discontinued contact and support.

Braver's survey strongly suggested that the biggest emphasis in developing cooperative postdivorce parenting should be on convincing mothers not to follow their impulse, egged on by their network, to "get this guy out of your life." So many women fail to understand this causal link between involvement and child support because nobody helps them see the obvious: the more they work with their ex-husbands in raising the kids, the easier their lives are going to be.

Now for the final recommendation, the truly mind-boggling concept of not fighting over what you pay her. When I was divorced, my French father gave me the typical male-to-male advice—"Go get laid"—and then shook his head, threw his hands apart in that famous way the Gauls have of shaking off fate, and repeated the old French axiom, "A father is a banker provided by nature."

I know it's difficult to accept this idea of yourself as the banker, especially when you no longer live with this woman. I recognize too that divorced men get slammed financially all the time. When you think about it, though, being nature's wallet isn't necessarily a bad thing for a man to be. It's really just modern civilization's version of division of labor. Our job as males is still to hunt, only now we bring home money instead of mastodon steaks.

So we all ought to be a little more conciliatory about this subject. Money is the root of almost all truly serious disagreements between ex-spouses, and in fact is a prime cause of divorce in the first place. I'm not suggesting you should accept having to eat out of tin cans, or let your ex-wife use your money for a jaunt to the Hawaiian islands instead of buying clothes for the kids, but if she's a halfway decent mother—and chances are she is—everything you do to make her life easier helps your children as well.

I know many of us are absolutely flattened by unjust and injurious child support and alimony payments, such as the shameless California support regulations. Those should be fought every time. On the other hand, there's no such thing as a free divorce, is there? If you're paying about half your take-home pay in child support and alimony combined, you are about at the norm. The conventional formula orders divorced dads to pay about 20 percent of their net income, give or take a few percentage points, for one child; anywhere from 30 percent to 35 percent for two kids, and as much as 45 percent for three. And that doesn't include alimony.

In most instances, money need not be grounds for a vicious and damaging court fight. Nor is it a reason for manipulative and dishonorable tactics like negotiating additional visitation time just to get reduced support payments. That's not another wild accusation by anti-dad feminists—in California, even fathers' divorce lawyers will tell you that kind of family law horse trading is prevalent. The tactic plays mind games not only with your ex, which is sure to incite hostility, but also with your kid, which is infinitely worse.

Similarly, I recommend that you agree to cover your kids under your company's health insurance policy. According to the government, only about 40 percent of parents with child support awards in 1992 had health insurance benefits included in their award, and 31 percent of the noncustodial parents who were required to provide these benefits in 1991 as part of the award failed to do so. Only 18 percent of noncustodial parents not required to provide these benefits as part of the award did so anyway.

Yes, that costs you money, but it's a small price to pay for your kids' health, let alone your right to stay involved in your kids' life, which is what happens when you provide their healthcare no matter who has primary custody.

One dad I interviewed didn't begrudge the child support he sent to his ex, but he did want to be sure the money was really being spent on his son.

"Once, when Billy was maybe four years old," says Jeff, "he got in my car and said, 'Mom told me to tell you I need a haircut, a new pair of jeans, and school shoes.' So we bought all those things and I deducted the cost from her next check. She went ballistic. I told her, 'I send you a check to do all these things. I shouldn't be asked to pay you and do this too.' She hasn't asked me to do it since."

The *Murphy Brown* Shirts

Former vice president Dan Quayle's attack on the single mom lifestyle TV show *Murphy Brown* was ridiculed during the 1992 presidential campaign, but revisionist commentators have since dragged it up again. "Quayle was right!" say these pundits, meaning that non nuclear parenting is doomed to fail. If divorce is the great villain, then the perpetrators of divorce, male as well as female, are also villainous.

Certainly the hysterical search for deadbeat dads (many if not most of whom are unmarried young men, by the way, and not divorced) has created sympathy for single moms that single dads don't enjoy. Still, custodial mothers are more often the object of pity than admiration. And they also are under attack by those who claim that one-parent families herald the death of our nation. That shrill warning ignores history, of course: single-parent families were more common in the nineteenth century than they are today, albeit because of death, rather than divorce, and our society managed to stumble into the twentieth century anyway.

Moreover, your divorced parenting challenges are more similar to what your ex-wife is facing than you might think. Custodial moms as well as noncustodial dads' relationships with their kids can be hurt by emotional distance. In her battle to build a new life, a custodial mother's economic situation often compels her to learn a new skill, reenter the job force, or spend more time on her current job. That's all time taken away from her kids, and kids need their mom just as much as they need their dad. It may not be as clear-cut as the loss of "father presence" because the kids live with their mother, but they feel it and react to it nonetheless.

Parenting Makes Strange (Former) Bedfellows

If there is any way for you to reduce the emotional charge between yourself and your ex-wife, you must do so. I know from happy experience that when two divorced parents act in concert for their children's benefit, they almost always win. When a camp counselor, daycare provider, teacher, or therapist needs to talk about Alex, *both* of us walk into that meeting, and we work together to pound out an agreed-upon course of action.

How nice for the Feuer family, you're thinking, but *your* ex-wife is a banshee. You could never do that.

Not true. My relationship with my ex is no different from yours. Too often she and I take perverse pleasure in pushing each other's buttons. We act petty and vindictive. I've been accused of emotional abuse; she's been accused of trying to drive a wedge between my son and me. We've had at least three or four breakdowns in which we screamed and yelled and humiliated each other in front of Alex. But we keep on keeping on. If we slip, we correct ourselves, learn from our mistakes, and move on, a couple divided and happy to keep it that way, but united nevertheless in a commitment to good parenting.

So walk a mile in your ex-wife's shoes. You'll be amazed at how much you'll learn.

Afterword:
Renewal and Looking to the Future

> To regret past mistakes is not as good as preventing
> future errors.
>
> —HUANCHU DAOREN, *REFLECTIONS ON THE TAO*

One of my hobbies is studying the paranormal—ghosts, near-death experiences, miracles, that sort of thing. Believe it or not, there are striking similarities, at least psychologically, between what happens to divorced dads and what happens to people who have paranormal experiences.

In my explorations of the unexplainable, I never cease to be amazed at how similar "alternate reality" experiences are, regardless of which culture they take place in or what fantastic explanation is given for them. Sudden drops in temperature. Loss of time. Strange, enigmatic beings speaking in riddles. Bright light. Whether we're talking about God appearing before Moses, Catholic miracles, meetings with leprechauns, ghostly hauntings, or close encounters with extraterrestrials, the list is always the same.

Now, no one really knows what these experiences are or what they mean, not even the scientists who study them or the religious leaders who interpret them. But we have been able to determine that two factors link most, if not all, of these experiences. First, they occur when people are facing a great or even life-threatening crisis and are under unbelievable emotional stress. Sometimes, of course, that stress is induced by the experience itself. Second, we know that whatever their circumstances, people who experience these strange happenings are permanently changed by them in the same way.

There's something primeval about these visits to what the Orange Catholic Bible calls "another world all around us," and for good reason; they're all versions of the Quest myth that is one of our most ancient ideas and appears in the stories of every human society. The Quest can be physical, mental, spiritual, or a combination of all three.

In the West, the Quest is undertaken by a hero or heroine (he or she has many names—Ulysses, Luke Skywalker, Robin Hood, Rocky, Bilbo Baggins, Alice in Wonderland, and countless others). The journey is born out of crisis, some circumstance or circumstances that present the protagonist with a challenge that rocks the whole universe and, in some stories, even destroys the world the protagonist knows. The journey tests abilities and emotions to the breaking point, but in the end, the hero emerges wiser, stronger, braver—better.

Divorce is rarely mystical, but no one comes through the experience unchanged. However and whenever it happens, divorce is a turning point in your personal myth, your trial by fire: the beginning of your individual Quest. You probably won't experience any sudden drops in temperature, encounter enigmatic beings who speak in riddles, or suffer time loss (although on plenty of occasions you may think you're going crazy). But you will be tested as you've never been tested before.

Divorce ends the life you knew. The quality of the new life you build depends to a large degree on how well you learn the lessons of your personal, divorce-created Quest. If you meet this daunting challenge, build a good life for yourself and your children, you will be a stronger, wiser, braver, better man.

Will, the dad who tried to handle his divorce by keeping his emotions barricaded behind a mental wall, says he learned from his particular Quest how critical it is to communicate. He thought if he protected his kids from his pain, he'd be able to keep them from feeling any of their own pain. But he learned that the kids needed to talk about the divorce even more than he did, since it was such a shock to them. His biggest mission now is teaching the benefits of communication to his kids, and he and his second wife spend most of their talking time discussing how they can get their kids to open up and express their feelings.

Nobody is only *slightly* affected by divorce. Either you experience an epiphany or you suffer a tragedy, or both. If you've done it right, you may find that you're not the only one who has walked through the fire. Your former wife has also gone on a Quest, and she also may have learned a thing or two.

One day Gary's ex-wife left him a message on his answering machine. She'd been watching videotapes of him playing with their two boys just before their marriage broke up.

"You know, you could see the stress on your face," she told him. "Our separating was the best thing that could have happened, and it's so much better now. We have common cause. It's like falling in love except we're focused on these two little human beings instead of each other. And when you do that, it's amazing the love you get back. I never thought it would turn out like this."

The Slow Creep of Reform

It's all so new, this divorce game. Seven years ago, my lawyer, a seasoned veteran of the uncivil war, with one thousand divorces under his belt, didn't even think to suggest a custody arrangement other than the traditional Tender Years concept of limited visitation. I didn't think to ask. My therapist didn't know where to direct me for postdivorce parenting help. My ex had only a vague notion that she shouldn't come between her son and his father. Alex, of course, just wanted everything to be the way it was. And my marriage broke up in California, mind you, supposedly the most progressive family law state in the nation (at least it used to be before the dark day the Golden State decided to screw around with child support payments).

Today, only a few years later, a newly divorced father has a multitude of places to turn to for help. There are programs pre-, during, and postdivorce for both divorcing parents. There are groups for the kids. There are online services. There are lobbying groups in Washington, encounter groups in the Midwest, Parents Without Partners dances everywhere.

And it's still not enough.

The demand continues to swell like a tidal wave. Divorce Online gets one thousand visits a week and e-mail messages from readers around the world (probably even some from the newly divorce-legal nation of Ireland). The Family Resource Center fields fifty calls a week from distressed or perplexed divorced dads.

And it's still not enough.

By even the most conservative estimates, a quarter of a million fathers become divorced dads in the United States every year. The need for research into the realities, attitudes, and problems of nonmarried fathers remains acute, and studies that deign to talk to the male parent are still rare enough that they continue to be described as "landmark," "groundbreaking," or "unique."

There are still far too few groups to handle the day-to-day challenges of being a divorced dad. The Tender Years Doctrine may be officially dead, but it lives on like a morbid shadow in the attitudes and practices of family law experts and divorced parents themselves. If you live in one of the more progressive states, you might be able to achieve some semblance of equality in your divorce parenting arrangement. In far too many others, however, you're still at the mercy of family values fascism or holy warrior feminists.

Dean Hughson gets e-mail pleas for help every day from men in Georgia, Alabama, Kentucky, Florida, and other states who have been told by the judges in their custody cases that "women are the nurturers around here, bud." And one female therapist in Florida has apparently decided to make a career of testifying against fathers in custody cases around the nation. I'm sure that when the children involved in those disputes are adults, they will thank this tireless crusader for gender bias.

Renewal

One day at the end of 1990, a week before I left my house and officially began my post divorce life, my wife went out with my infant son to visit one of her friends. I sat in the kitchen and listened to the rain make drum solos on the roof. After a while, I got up and walked slowly from room to room, touching the walls, the photos of our life together, the toys in my little boy's room.

I felt like a ghost in my own home. And I wondered what would happen to the relationship between me and my son.

Two weeks later, as I was packing to move into my new apartment, my soon-to-be-ex-wife appeared in the doorway. By now, we were exhausted from the combat of divorce and, in a lull between accusations, we actually were civil to each other for a few minutes.

"Do you think you'll ever get married again?" she asked.

"Maybe," I said.

"Do you want more children?"

"I might."

Hearing this, she suddenly started to cry.

"If you do, will you forget Alex?" she asked in a quavering voice. "Will he have to take a backseat to your new children because you had him with me?"

That was the first time I realized, really realized, that she was feeling exactly what I was feeling. I knew then there are no winners in America's uncivil war. No heroes. No villains. Only human beings, struggling to do the right thing. There is no vindication, no glory, no righteousness. There is only the pain of broken dreams and the sad eyes of children searching for a reason.

Like all minorities, it is easy for divorced men to lose themselves in rage and frustration and strike back at their tormentors. But two wrongs never make a right.

Two parents, however, can always make a child whole.

To the Rescue:
Recommended Resources

My therapist wouldn't be as frustrated helping me find help
today as she was in 1990. Many fathers' rights groups have
found a greater voice and a higher profile in recent years.
She'd still be hard-pressed, however, to find a single comprehensive source of advice for divorced dads. Although
there are now resources available over the phone, through
the computer, in books and magazines, and from fathers'
rights organizations, no one person, place, or thing provides
all the help a divorced dad needs.

In fact, getting comprehensive advice on all aspects of divorced-dad parenting is a lot like ordering in a Chinese restaurant. You have to choose one from column A and one
from column B and create your own meal.

Since few resources are specific to a divorced dad's per-
spective but most offer at least general support for divorced
people, with new ones cropping up all the time, it's impossible to provide an all-inclusive listing of everything that's
out there. So the recommendations of where to turn provided

in this chapter are not the only resources available on the subject of divorce. I've chosen them because they provide one or more of the following: effective overall counsel or services to divorced parents; shortcuts to other lists of resources; or a specific dedication to the divorced dad's point of view.

Naturally, your search for support should not be limited to libraries or the Internet. Your church, synagogue, or mosque; divorced friends; and your doctor or therapist can refer you to other resources. And, of course, all the general parenting books, newspapers, and regional magazines will be helpful to you as well.

When you go looking for help, remember that patience is a virtue. Many of the themes running through this book are universal and appear virtually wherever there is discourse of any kind on nonmarried parenting. Issues like the effect of conflict between ex-spouses on kids, children blaming themselves for their parents' divorce, the dynamics of anger between divorced parents, and others are common to every divorced family. So everybody talks or writes about them.

Reactions to these ubiquitous challenges, however, are as varied as the individuals who face them. Good ideas on how to handle a particular situation can come from anywhere. So it pays to slog through yet another admonishment to minimize conflict with your ex-spouse, because the next thing you read might be a gem of a suggestion for reducing tension that you've never thought of before.

Finally, of course, be prepared to endure horror story after horror story about bad men and women doing terrible things to their ex-spouses and their kids. It's an uncivil war, remember? There are casualties on both sides. That should not discourage you from seeking help. Let it be, instead, inspiration for you to keep fighting for the right to be a good parent to your children.

By the Books

You'll never build a library of books by, about, or for divorced dads. You can count such treasures on the fingers of one hand, but they do exist. And several books on the general consequences of divorce are unanimously praised for their ability to help every man, woman, and child in a sundered family. (Since the literature on step-parenting is as voluminous as the body of work on divorce, no step-parenting books are included in these recommendations. However, every one of the general divorce books includes a chapter on step-parenting.)

• *Putting Kids First*, by Michael L. Oddenino (Family Connections Publishing, 1995). Besides the delicious symbolism of beginning a divorced-dad book list with one entitled *Putting Kids First*, this is a resource on divorced fathering by a divorced father—a rarity indeed. Moreover, this is not just any divorced father, but a guy who really understands the subject. Oddenino, a California divorce attorney, is also counsel for the Children's Rights Council. He is a remarkable dad, and this slim book overflows with anecdotes and advice that can help any good man be a better dad to his kids. If you buy any of the books on this list, choose this one.

• *The Parents Book About Divorce*, by Richard A. Gardner, M.D. (Bantam Books, 1977). Gardner, the psychologist who came up with the term "parent alienation syndrome," is one of the nation's most respected experts on the consequences of divorce on kids. This book is a follow-up to *The Boys and Girls Book About Divorce* and provides extremely useful insight into how divorce affects children of all ages. Like almost every other book written by a psychologist, it tends to be dry and wordy. But it is a must for your divorced-dad library.

• *Families Apart: Ten Keys to Successful Co-Parenting*, by Melinda Blau (Perigee, 1993). Because she is a journalist, Blau's writing style is easy to absorb. Because she is an expert on shared parenting—writing columns, books, and feature articles on the subject—she knows her stuff. Most important, though, because she is a divorced parent, she brings the insight of personal experience to the table. *Families Apart* is a fine treatise on how to cooperate with your ex for the good of the kids, and one of the few written by a woman that doesn't contain laugh-out-loud misperceptions of how divorced dads feel.

• *Mom's House, Dad's House*, by Isolina Ricci, Ph.D. (Collier Books, 1980). This book was recommended to me by several people and is referred to by other divorce authors, so you know it has some good advice in it. Indeed, *Mom's House* is an exhaustive blueprint for making joint custody work. That's fine—if you're a firm believer in the concept of two separate but equal homes for a child. Also, because she's a scientist, some of Ricci's ideas can be impractical in the real world of emotionally seared human beings, like a few of her suggestions for drawing up a parenting plan. Nevertheless, Ricci's book is a sturdy source of advice for divorced dads, filled with useful ideas for postdivorce parenting.

• *Growing Up With Divorce*, by Neil Kalter (Free Press, 1990). Kalter is also a famous psychiatrist specializing in divorce, and, like Gardner, he can be enormously useful in helping divorced dads understand how the breakup of their marriage may affect their kids, and what to do about it. Several researchers interviewed for *Good Men* paid homage to Kalter's work, one even calling him "the best expert" on the effects of divorce on children.

• *The Divorced Parent*, by Stephanie Marston (Pocket Books, 1994). The author is a therapist who has parlayed her expertise into appearances on talk shows and other trappings of success in the self-help business. That means the bulk of her readership is female, and she writes accordingly. Still, her book is easy to digest for divorced parents of either gender; its intent is not to show off the author's scientific acumen, but to communicate actionable information to ordinary people. And its focus—"how to nurture happy, well-adjusted children in a divorced family"—earns *The Divorced Parent* a spot on the recommended list.

• *Divorce Book for Parents*, by Vicki Lansky (New American Library, 1989). If Ann Landers, Erma Bombeck, and Dr. Joyce Brothers were fused together and wrote specifically on parenting, they'd be Vicki Lansky, columnist, author, Internet authority, and self-help cottage industry. Her style can be really annoying, especially to male readers, but don't let Lansky's blithe spirit fool you. The woman knows her stuff, and her *Divorce Book* is an exhaustive, authoritative, and easy-to-read reference on postdivorce parenting.

• *The Good Divorce*, by Constance R. Ahrons, Ph.D. (Harper-Collins, 1994). This book has gotten enormous play, and with good reason. Ahrons is excellent at offering suggestions on how to make shared parenting work. But she is a southern California therapist, and you can hear the influence of Hollywood in the many euphemisms she invents. Ahrons coined the phrase "binuclear family," for example, and she divides the various types of divorced-couple relationships (she calls them typologies) into sometimes goofy name groupings, like "Perfect Pals." Nevertheless, she is one of the few researchers committed to an inclusive study of divorced parenting: her subjects are both male and female parents, and she writes accordingly. For that reason alone, she is a valuable resource for divorced dads.

• *Custody for Fathers*, by Michael and Carleen Brennan (self-published, 1995). These divorce lawyers have written and self-published the definitive guide for fathers seeking custody of their kids. You want commitment from your divorced-dad resources? Carleen Brennan is so passionate about helping divorced dads that she broke down in tears while giving a speech on the subject. This book is only available at a few bookstores, so you may find it easier to order it from the Brennans themselves. Their numbers are (714) 646–3453 (fax) or (714) 646–9842 (office).

• *Will They Love Me When I Leave? A Weekend Father's Struggle to Stay Close to His Kids*, by C. W. Smith (Putnam, 1987). A screenwriter friend of mine dug up a copy of this book from the back shelves of his personal library and gave it to me. He told me that Smith's story would blow me away, and he wasn't kidding. It's well worth a trip to the library to find a copy. Smith, a heralded journalist and novelist, has written a profoundly honest and visceral account of his experiences as a noncustodial—and distant—divorced dad. It is an extraordinary book and, as far as I can discern, the only one of its kind.

• *Single Fatherhood*, by Chuck Gregg, Ph.D. (Sulzburger & Graham, 1995). The author is a professor of educational psychology at the University of Utah, who raised three kids—two boys and a girl—by himself for fifteen years. Although this resource isn't aimed specifically at *divorced* fathers, it covers many topics that will interest divorced dads, like child-proofing the furniture, feeding kids properly, handling emotions, even what to bring in the car on a road trip. Not surprisingly, given its author's profession, the style of *Single Fatherhood* is dry and scholarly, but nonetheless it's crammed full of useful stuff.

• *Divorced Dads*, by C. Stephen Fouquet (Fairview Press, 1996). I include this book simply because the fathers whose stories it tells are all divorced dads. There are so few books specifically about us that every one of them deserves mention. *Divorced Dads*, however, goes far beyond the experience of the average divorced dad. Of the nineteen stories contained herein, several are of dads whose kids are HIV positive; one is a gay dad; one is a father serving a prison term for murdering his last wife; and another is taking his kids because his ex-wife is dying.

The Organization Man

One group invariably leads to another, so although there are only a handful of organizations listed here, good men can access almost any other fathers' rights or family movement in America through them. These are particularly useful or wield greater than average clout.

• *Children's Rights Council*, 220 I Street NE, Suite 230, Washington, D.C. 20002–4362. Phone: (202) 547–6227 (headquarters); (202) 546–4272 (fax). The CRC is a powerful national children's rights organization, probably the most successful fathers' rights lobbying group in the country. There are CRC chapters in more than half of the states, giving it comprehensive insight into the vagaries of divorce law in the United States. The CRC's mandate is extremely broad, encompassing every conceivable kind of parent, including married ones, and it is unabashedly political. Its main focus, therefore, is on influencing custody and visitation legislation. The organization is a tireless defender of the right of every child to two parents, which by definition makes it a stalwart ally of divorced dads. Moreover, CRC's support materials include books, videos, and resource guides on every conceivable kind of parenting problem or challenge—including a priceless "parenting directory" that lists organizations by state. The CRC's relatively meager annual dues—$35 as of 1997—is the best investment a divorced dad can make.

• *Parents Without Partners*, 401 North Michigan Avenue, Chicago, IL 60611–4267. Phone: (312) 644–6610 (headquarters);

(312) 321–6969 (fax). This is the second place a divorced dad should turn after calling the CRC. Parents Without Partners is a one-stop social resource for single parents, offering encounter groups, parent/kid trips, dances, and many other services. It's a great group, very upbeat, and its events are a lot of fun. There are PWP chapters everywhere; divorced dads ought to begin a search for the PWP chapter closest to them simply by dialing information.

• *Joint Custody Association*, 10606 Wilkins Avenue, Los Angeles, CA 90024. Phone: (301) 475–5352. This group spearheads the growing joint-custody movement in the United States. It provides members with a truckload of background information on joint custody and regularly lobbies on behalf of single fathers.

• *Academy of Family Mediators*, 1500 South Highway 100, Suite 355, Golden Valley, MN 55416. Phone: (612) 525–8670 (headquarters); (612) 525–8725 (fax). Although this is a professional organization, divorced or divorcing fathers who are interested in the growing mediation movement can call or write the academy for background and other information on what mediation is and what it does, what kind of costs to expect, and how to find a mediator.

• *Fathers' Resource Center*, 430 Oak Grove Street, Suite B3, Minneapolis, MN 55403. Phone: (612) 874–1509 (headquarters); (612) 874–0221 (fax). This is a local group, but a very good one, and it happily helps anybody who calls. The FRC's focus is on good fathering, no matter what the marital situation is, and it provides a healthy number of resources for good men. Its courses on how to handle anger are particularly good.

• *National Congress for Men and Children, Communication and Data Center*, P.O. Box 6053, Kansas City, KS 66106–0053. Phone: (800) 733–DADS. Previously just the National Congress for Men, this is also a useful organization to contact on legal matters and advice on how to handle custody and visitation issues.

• *The Stepfamily Foundation*, 333 West End Avenue, New York, NY 10023. Phone: (212) 877–3244 (headquarters); (212) 362–7030 (fax). This organization has been around for some time, and it is included here because of its willingness to counsel good men over the phone. A very good resource for those ticklish remarriage situations.

Logging On

The Interactive Age has opened new electronic avenues for divorced dads. Cyberhelp is available on virtually every issue you may face in your postdivorce parenting.

The explosion of cyberservices has spawned a proliferating group of fathers' rights home pages. Most of these sites are oriented to legal issues, while others are nothing more than a bunch of divorced guys sitting in front of their computers typing woe-is-me complaints to one another. Nevertheless, there are several real gold mines for postdivorce parenting, home pages or just lists of organizations, written by and for divorced dads. Moreover, each one of the fathers' rights home pages is linked to many others offering conversation, counsel, or divorced-dad products and services.

• One very useful new electronic avenue for postdivorce parenting help is *Divorce Online magazine* on the Internet at http://www.divorce-online.com. Edited and produced by professionals specializing in divorce, this e-mag regularly features interviews by experts on legal, psychological, and other issues affecting divorced parents.

• Divorced dads also get together in cyberspace and talk about their lives on the *FREE home page* (Fathers' Rights and Equality Exchange), http : / / www. info-sys. home. vix. com/free/. This organization is a very active and supportive one that works mostly with divorced dads. FREE specializes in providing divorced fathers with legal pointers or steering them to lawyers, but its home page also provides links to other Web sources.

Annie Mitchell, lawyer and founder of FREE, is usually not available through e-mail, but you will get a programmed response that will direct you to other resources. Mitchell's e-mail address is shedevil@vix.com.

• *Dean Hughson*, the online divorced dad expert, offers the Divorce Page at http://hughson.com/, which gives you access to a broad range of services and support resources, from custody and other legal issues to divorce and religion. You also can e-mail Hughson at dean@primenet.com. He's the best of the online experts at responding to inquiries, and he's a great resource for other phone numbers, organizations, and divorced-dad help tips.

Since Web site addresses change frequently, don't be surprised or frustrated if some of the Internet addresses I've provided are outdated by the time this book reaches you. Even if they have changed locations, many of these Web services, sites, and sources can be tracked down with the keywords fathers' rights or divorce through search engines such as Lycos or Yahoo! and through online services such as America Online, CompuServe, and Prodigy. And, of course, most of them are linked to one another, so you can access one and surf many of the others to your cyberheart's content.

Index